Be More Owl

Life Lessons from
Our Feathered
Friends

Alison Davies

Be More Owl

Life Lessons from Our Feathered Friends

Illustrations by Emily Mayor

Contents

Introduction 6

Chapter One
Discover the Beauty in Silence 10

Chapter Two
Find Your Own Voice 28

Chapter Three
Listen With Intent 46

Chapter Four
See the Bigger Picture 64

Chapter Five
Let Intuition Be Your Guide 84

Chapter Six
Embrace the Darkness 102

Chapter Seven
Release What No Longer Serves You 122

About the Author 142
Acknowledgements 143

Introduction

Owls are enigmatic and they look the part. Their large, glistening eyes pierce the night and exude an ethereal wisdom. They move seamlessly, these creatures of land and air, often taking to the skies when we're at slumber, vast **wings gliding gracefully** over hill and dale and through a myriad of other landscapes. Owls come in all shapes and sizes, but the one thing they have in common is a curious expression and a sense of knowing that seems to go beyond the veil. These birds are mystical in form and habit. No wonder the ancients were mesmerized, believing that they had been touched by something otherworldly. Their effortless flight and ability to disappear, melting into the backdrop of a starry night, gave them a magical aura. Couple this with an eerie cry, issued under sheath of darkness, and this was proof enough that there was something supernatural afoot. Stories abound of owl omens – prophecies carried on the tip of a wing during the **WITCHING HOUR**.

Today we know the truth behind these natural wonders. We understand that they are uniquely gifted. Their dextrous wings allow them to fly **swiftly and soundlessly**, and their eyes help pinpoint the tiniest flicker of movement in

the undergrowth. Their ears transmit sound in a unique way, helping them to create a 3D picture of the landscape, and if this wasn't enough, strong, sturdy talons provide them with all they need to secure a late-night snack – no fuss, no messing. Service is quick and efficient, giving a whole new meaning to 'fast food'. Once the food is digested, the small bones are smoothly ejected in a pellet, making space for something new. But it's the behaviour of these birds that really sets them apart from the avian crowd.

Owls are the silent sentinels of the animal kingdom. There's no need to rush when you're cosied up within a leafy tree branch. Time moves slowly for these gifted birds. While we may rush around trying to fit ten thousand things into our day, the owl knows that **there is power in patience**. Here it sits in serenity, assessing the situation and allowing it to unfold. There's no need to stretch for what is clearly above you. This bird takes a different approach and uses its perception effectively, listening and reaching into the night with all of its senses. Only when it has the full picture will it make a move. There's nothing hasty about the wise owl. Intuition is where it's at and the subtle sixth sense is always at work, scouring the land and looking for clues to help this bird survive and thrive.

There is much to take under the wing and fully digest when watching an owl **DO ITS THING**. Whether you're fascinated by the way they look and their nocturnal habits, or interested in the folklore and the mystical reputation of this sharp-eyed beauty, you will find an array of interesting facts and features within these pages. You will come to understand that there is more to this avian than meets the eye, and that given time you can follow suit and harness these gifts yourself. You will become enchanted by this mystery cloaked in feathers and grow to appreciate the skills at play and the owlish way that you can benefit. The beautiful illustrations will help you connect with this bird at a deeper level, and the exercises and tips within will give you all you need to succeed. All that's left to say is enjoy discovering what makes this bird tick. Take your time, take a moment and, when you're ready, **take flight and be more owl**.

Chapter One
Discover the Beauty in Silence

'A wise old owl lived in an oak. The more he saw, the less he spoke. The less he spoke, the more he heard. Why can't we all be like that bird?'

Edward Hersey Richards

Masters of disguise, owls are the spies of the avian kingdom, able to blend into their surroundings at the blink of a watchful eye. This gives them the upper wing when it comes to spotting the next meal or concealing their whereabouts from a hungry predator.

Each unique species is gifted with a plumage to match its environment. The burrowing owl is a prime example, staying low to the ground where its sandy mottled feathers blend seamlessly into the prairie desert, while the screech owl makes its eerie call, wearing a uniform of deep red to match the coniferous trees it haunts. Snowy owls melt into the Arctic tundra thanks to their ivory whiteness, and the buff tawny hues of barn owls make it easy for them to disappear in the farmland they favour. Couple this with the head tufts, which appear like ears but are in fact feathers adapted to look like twigs, and you have a trick of the eye that puts top-tech Bond gadgets to shame. But what is the reason for all of this subterfuge? Do these secretive birds have something to hide, or is something else afoot?

Fledging owlets do well to watch their elders before they find their feathers, for this camouflage only works when the owl is motionless. **Stillness is the real secret of their success.** The ability to sit and appraise the situation without the need to take action is where the magic lies. Being in the moment keeps them present, meaning those

Discover the Beauty in Silence

wide eyes and sharp ears never miss a trick or the flick of an insect's wing. These awesome avians watch and wait as time stands still, then in an instant they are off, vast wings launching into the air, ready to make the most of an opportunity. Seize the day and the prey. It matters not to the canny owl, who knows only one way to be – open in heart and mind and shrouded in tranquillity.

Silent flight is the superpower that allows them to propel forwards and act upon any perceived chance. Their large wings encourage **SLOW, STEADY MOVEMENT** with less flapping, while their comb-like serrated edges

act as silencers, breaking up the air to reduce noise. The resulting hush is nature's lullaby – or perhaps, an omen of danger for the small creatures of the night.

This is a bird that goes gently. It knows that true power comes not in charging forth with bluster, but in maintaining an air of calm and assessing the situation from afar. Only then can it truly see what counts and make a decision from which to move with grace.

No fast and furious takeaway here. The owl's laid-back approach to late-night snacking guarantees success and a full tum. **STILLNESS** and **SILENCE** are the **SECRET WEAPONS** it conceals beneath its wings and they can work for us too, helping us find peace and balance when we're under stress. While we may not need to hunt for our dinner, we do need to survive and thrive in the world around us, and that requires patience and the **ability to live in the moment**.

Serenity can be our sanctuary, just as the owl finds solace and safety in those quiet moments when it **blends into obscurity**. This bird's path to inner calm is about being rather than doing, letting external noise fade away and allowing the soft, soundless majesty of nature to envelop the soul.

Be More Owl

Take some time in your day to camouflage. Simply stop what you're doing, take a long, deep breath and sit in stillness. Imagine you're an owl perched within a tree. From this spot, you can see everything going on around you, but rather than acting or interacting with anything or anyone, you're going to watch and wait and let your surroundings envelop you. If it helps, give yourself a time limit. For example, you might want to set a timer on your phone for two minutes. During this time, try not to get drawn into doing anything. Breathe deeply and take in everything you can see. Notice the little things that might normally escape your field of vision. Consider also what you can hear and feel, but don't let yourself get drawn into anything: simply notice the noises floating around you. Let thoughts flow through your mind and try not to focus on any one thing. Instead, bring your attention back to your breathing and let the world carry on around you until the two minutes are up.

Discover the Beauty in Silence

Stillness Meditation

It's not easy to be still. Owls do this naturally, but we are programmed to be active and juggle many things at once. To embrace the power of stillness, make space in your schedule after a busy day to practise this short meditation.

Try this!

You will need
Cushions, throws, candles

🌿 To begin, find somewhere that you can sit, preferably on the floor, where you won't be disturbed. Switch off all electrical devices and arrange cushions and throws to ensure you are comfortable and your back is supported.

🌿 Light the candles to create a soothing atmosphere.

🌿 Push your bottom into the floor to help ground you, and lengthen your spine. Roll your shoulders back to relieve any tension that you've stored during the day.

🌿 Close your eyes and take a deep breath in. Imagine you're drawing it up through your body from the ground.

🍂 Hold the breath in your chest for a little longer than you would normally, then release it slowly through your mouth. Continue to breathe in this way for a couple of minutes to calm your mind.

🍂 As you sit, picture a stream in the middle of a wood. Look at the glistening surface of the tranquil water and notice how still it seems, despite the fact that it is moving towards a destination.

🍂 Imagine you are like this water. You flow with the movement of your breath, while remaining motionless in thought and mind. It doesn't matter what is happening in the outside world, you are sheltered here, able to sit in stillness and silence.

🍂 As you inhale, imagine you're drawing in the stillness, the pure energy of nature.

🍂 As you breathe out, feel it flowing from you like a stream.

🍂 If any thoughts pop into your head, acknowledge them, then return to your breathing and the stream in the woods.

🍂 Try and maintain this stillness for at least five minutes. As you practise this meditation more, you can extend the length of time so that eventually you can sit in stillness for 30 minutes and really feel the benefits of this inner peace.

Be More Owl

Owls go it alone. They don't need external stimulation clogging up their senses. They know that the night is sacred, a time to restore and heal beneath a blanket of darkness. Owls immerse themselves in the natural world and let this soothe them into a serene state. Take inspiration from our feathered friends and disconnect from the high-tech world by switching off all of your devices at least an hour before bed – this includes smart phones, tablets, laptops and even the TV. Give your brain time to relax, and your eyes a chance to soften and become accustomed to the dimming light. Instead of scrolling through endless posts and reels, gaze out of the window and take in the view. Even if you can't see much through the veil of night, let the backdrop calm you. Look up at the sky and notice the pattern of the stars and the light of the moon. Breathe, and absorb the stillness.

Owl Spotlight

Snowy Owl

Also known as the polar or Arctic owl, this striking bird has **SNOWY WHITE FEATHERS**, as the name suggests, although the females' plumage is often peppered with black and brown flecks. Large and muscular, the snowy owl has **bright yellow eyes** and a black beak. Nesting out on the tundra, this bird will peruse the icy vista along **SHORELINES**, **MARSHES** and **LAKESIDES** in search of small rodents to feast upon. It is native to the Arctic regions of North America and the Palaearctic.

The Sound of Silence

It can be a challenge to spend any amount of time in complete silence, but the benefits are bountiful. Removing outside stimulation makes space for something new and allows you to really connect with yourself. It renews body and mind and triggers your creative brain. It also helps with focus and clarity.

Just as the owl sits in stillness, its senses primed for action, when you **immerse yourself in the sound of silence**, you experience the world at a deeper level. That said, it's not always easy to find the time to do this: work, home life and all of the many commitments that take precedence mean that silence can be hard to find. Try the following steps to connect with the quiet in your life.

Step One

Set your alarm earlier in the morning, to allow yourself five minutes of complete silence to acclimatize to the day and gather your thoughts. Don't be in a rush to do anything during this time. Be still and quiet, and let yourself adjust.

Step Two

Create a sanctuary in your home where you can go and be alone. It doesn't matter where this space is. It could be your garden or the bedroom. Make it clear to those you live with that this is your space and a place where you go for peace.

Step Three

Every week, go for a walk in nature and immerse yourself in the landscape. While you won't be in complete silence, the sounds of nature have a soothing effect on the mind. Try and tune out other noise so that you can appreciate the little things, like the rustle of the wind through the trees and the sound of birdsong.

Step Four

Stop at least once a day and take yourself to a quiet spot. Place both hands over your heart. Breathe deeply and listen the sound of your own body. Notice the tempo of each breath, and slow this down. Feel the peace envelop you.

Step Five

Challenge yourself to spend half a day where you don't speak to anyone. Use the silence to connect with yourself, and to what really counts, so you might spend the time doing something creative, or journalling.

Be More Owl

Owls make their home in nature, from those that burrow in the ground to the tree dwellers who find the perfect crevice or crooked branch within a sturdy trunk to nestle. Follow suit and let Mother Nature ground you by having a moment of stillness, barefoot upon the grass. Press your soles deep into the earth and feel the connection that you have with the natural world. Feel the blades of grass pushing up between your toes and revel in the coolness of their touch. Draw a long, deep breath in through the soles of each foot and imagine it travelling up through your body, into your chest.

As you exhale, picture tiny strands of root extending from each foot, deep into the ground. These roots hold you in place, anchoring you to the earth. Relax and embrace the peace and balance of this quiet moment.

Star Bathing

Owls are expert **STAR GAZERS**. These wise wonders favour the stillness of night to hunt and be at one with the world. You too can experience this joy and connect with the magic of a starry sky by sitting quietly and looking up.

🪶 **It helps if you have a good viewing spot.** The top of a hill is perfect, but a comfy chair in the garden works just as well, as long as you can see the sky clearly.

🪶 **Make sure you are warm and comfortable.** Cocoon yourself in blankets and get into a position where you are relaxed.

🪶 **Breathe deeply** and let your gaze soften as you look up at the stars.

🪶 **Notice any shapes or patterns that stand out.** Use your imagination and make pictures in your mind.

🪶 **Listen to the sounds** that surround you.

🪶 **Relax** and enjoy the experience.

🪶 **Feel** the velvety blanket of the night sky wrap around you, bringing stillness and calm.

Owl Magic: Lavender Sleep Ritual

Sleep comes easily to the night owl, who has learned to prowl under the cover of darkness. Being mostly nocturnal, a daily dose of **ZZZS** is essential, but while shut-eye may evade you, this bird knows that the secret to a doze comes in still, silent repose. Follow this feathered beauty's regime, and **slip seamlessly into dreams** by sprinkling lavender essential oil upon your pillow. Invest in a soft, cosy eye mask and add a drop of the oil on the outer side, while making a wish for a restful night. Then cocoon yourself in the covers and imagine you're enveloped in a cloak of owl feathers. Still, quiet and calm...

OWL AFFIRMATIONS

I embrace the solace of silence.

Stillness envelops me; I am cocooned in calm.

I breathe in peace; I breathe out stress and tension.

I sit in stillness; safe, secure and present.

The quiet of the night is a soothing blanket around my shoulders.

No need to rush or act, this present moment of peace is all that counts.

Chapter Two
Find Your Own Voice

'The little owls call to each other with tremulous, quavering voices throughout the livelong night, as they sit in the creaking trees.'

Theodore Roosevelt

Each distinctive species of owl has its own signature **tune, hook and look**, making for a truly diverse and expressive parliament when gathered together. There's nothing bland about a band of owls, for while you might think they're all about the hoot, there's also a fluting toot, a **SCREECH,** a cat-like miaow and various whistles, bristles and equine whinnies to add to this orchestra of sound. Indeed, owls are incredibly expressive when push comes to shove during the breeding season, but even in quieter periods they've been known to call out or shout of their whereabouts. After all, these denizens of the night have a reputation to uphold.

The blood-curdling screams of the barn owl are reason enough to **hide beneath the covers**, but take comfort in knowing that the purpose behind this haunting call is less fear-fuelled frenzy and more likely infused with longing. As the veil of midnight takes hold, the charming male becomes bold and ready to woo his mate, and so the concert of courtship begins as feathered amours screech from the rafters in a bid to secure a bond. And afterwards, when love has blossomed, the voracious call is a way to keep other male suitors at bay. They may be 'Birds of omen, dark and foul', according to Sir Walter Scott, but this evil reputation was hearsay, and not at all the way of the owl.

Each to their own when it comes to communication, for these birds know that you don't have to **sound the same** to show that you're a **part of the team**. Short-eared owls speak with a barky rasp, and some females even favour a chicken-like cluck as they woo their love. Boreal owls and screech owls are fans of a high-pitched toot, as opposed to the hoary hoot of the tawny owl, which varies depending on where it hails from.

These clever birds have learned how to **ADAPT THEIR CALL** to reach a wider audience. When the landscape is dense and peppered with obstacles, they use a lower pitch, which is less likely to be lost among the trees. Similarly, if it's windy, they know that bass notes carry better along the breeze, while an open vista is an opportunity to show off the higher echelons of their vocal range.

Owls are adept at being heard when they need to get their message across. Whether defending their territory, attracting new love or simply making their presence known, these birds know the merits of good communication. And while most owls are generally solitary in nature, **they'll always look out for feathered friends** by warning them of nearby predators. After all, it doesn't take much to reach out and call your nearest and dearest – a truth we could all benefit from.

Unique in sound, unique in sight – owls are distinctly different in the way they look, too, but that's OK, because every owl worth its toot knows that you don't have to follow suit to make a lasting impression. Birds come in all shapes and sizes – and just like humans, each one is special in its own unique way. Some are pale and slender like the graceful barn owl, while others are compact and bijou like the little owl. The tawny owl is deeply mottled, with broad wings with a greyish, reddish tint, while the eagle owl, with its stocky body and **ENORMOUS WINGSPAN**, commands respect. Each one has its strengths and talents, and expresses itself with passion, a lesson we too can learn if we want to earn our place in the pecking order.

Whatever way we choose to express ourselves, there is much to gain from watching our feathered friends navigate the world around them. We can take inspiration from their unique calls and **find our own voice**. By learning how to communicate more effectively with others, we can discover how to be confident and creative in every aspect of our lives. Most importantly, we can understand that being true to ourselves is the only way to live a happy, fulfilling and successful life.

Be More Owl

Being true to yourself means acknowledging who you are and how you feel at any given moment. Owls can't change their feathers, and they wouldn't want to! Each type of owl is uniquely gifted and equipped to deal with their environment, just as you have all the tools you need to excel, once you accept your truth in the present moment. Be more owl and get into the habit of checking in with yourself throughout the day. Take a minute to sit, breathe and be present in your body. Ask yourself, 'How do I feel right now, in this moment?' Scan each body part and acknowledge any feelings of tension or stress, any heaviness or tightness. If you find any areas that feel like this, breathe into them and relax the muscles. Imagine that your breath is infused with healing light that travels around your body to soothe any parts of you that feel off-kilter. Consider how you are feeling in yourself: do you feel happy, sad, angry, frustrated, excited? It doesn't matter which emotion governs your thoughts, simply acknowledge it, be aware of it, then let it flow through you like an owl in flight.

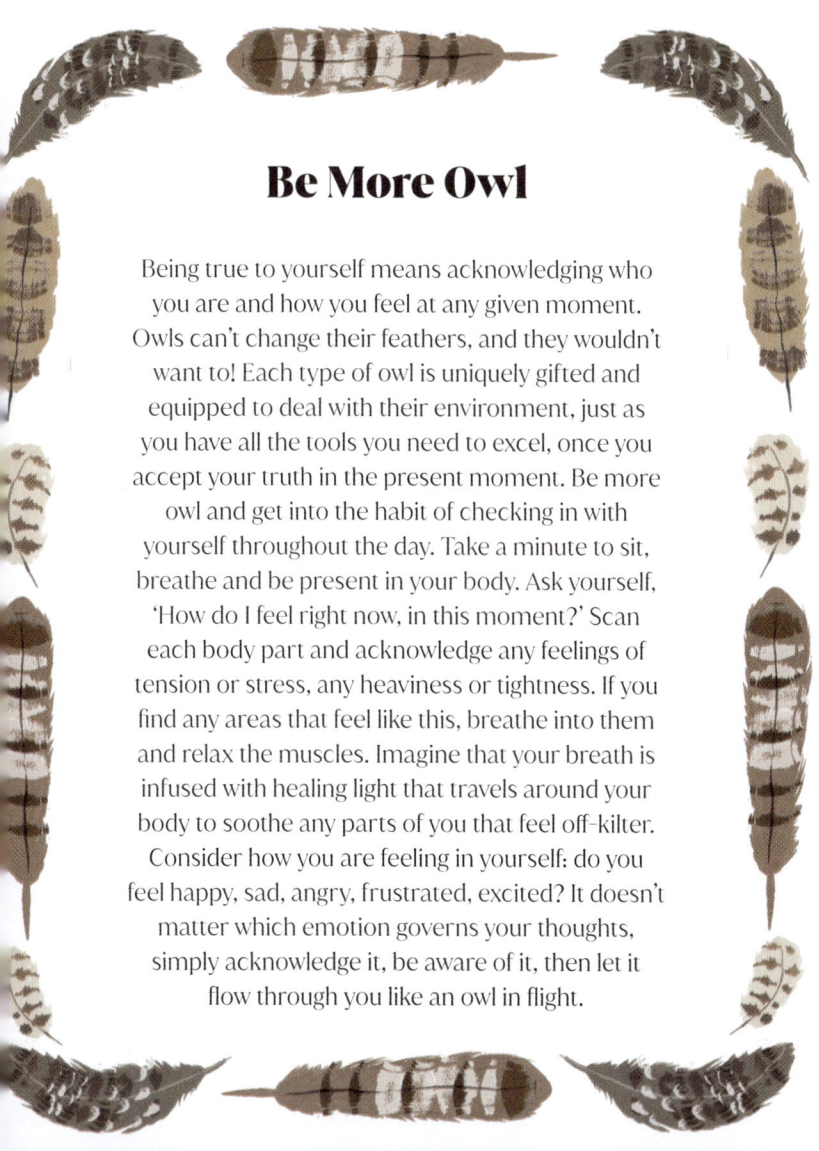

Find Your Call

Are you a **TOOTER** or a **HOOTER**? Perhaps you'd prefer to growl, or even howl, at the night. The choice is yours. Owls communicate in various ways, with each species favouring a different type of call, but that's OK because it's all about finding the best and most creative way to **express yourself**. You can do the same, by following your heart and experimenting with different types of communication.

Try this!

You will need:
A journal with some space to be creative and a pen.

🍂 Take some time to clear your mind before you begin. You might want to burn some scented oil and spend a few minutes breathing deeply to centre yourself.

🍂 When you're ready, open your journal to a blank page.

🍂 Consider what makes you feel happy and inspired. What would lift your spirits right now? Do you find joy in walking in nature, or perhaps you prefer the cosy comfort of a warm armchair and a good book? Let your thoughts flow as you mull over all of the possibilities.

🌿 If you could be anywhere in the world, where would you be?

🌿 Close your eyes and go to that special place in your mind. Take a walk around and experience it as if you've never been there before. Engage all of your senses and make it as real as possible.

🌿 Now open your eyes, and look at the page before you. Write, draw, doodle or sketch, do something to express how you feel in this moment.

🌿 You might want to draw an image to represent your special place or write a few words or a poem that communicates your feelings.

🌿 Let your creative mind take over and have fun exploring this side of yourself. Find your own unique way of communicating your thoughts and feelings. It doesn't matter if it's not perfect; this is about you engaging with your imagination and learning to express yourself creatively.

🌿 When you practise expressing yourself in this way, you stimulate your creative brain and this boosts confidence, which will help you to communicate more effectively on a daily basis.

Owl Spotlight

Tawny Owl

This woodland owl has a plump plumage and roundish body and head. Medium-sized overall, its large, dark eyes and hooked beak are encircled by a ring of dark feathers. Compact and powerful, it is a **VORACIOUS HUNTER**, favouring broadleaf and mixed woody areas. It can also be found in large urban parks, and occasionally will visit nearby gardens to hunt, though it will avoid built-up areas. Commonly found across Europe and western Siberia, the tawny has several subspecies.

Be More Owl

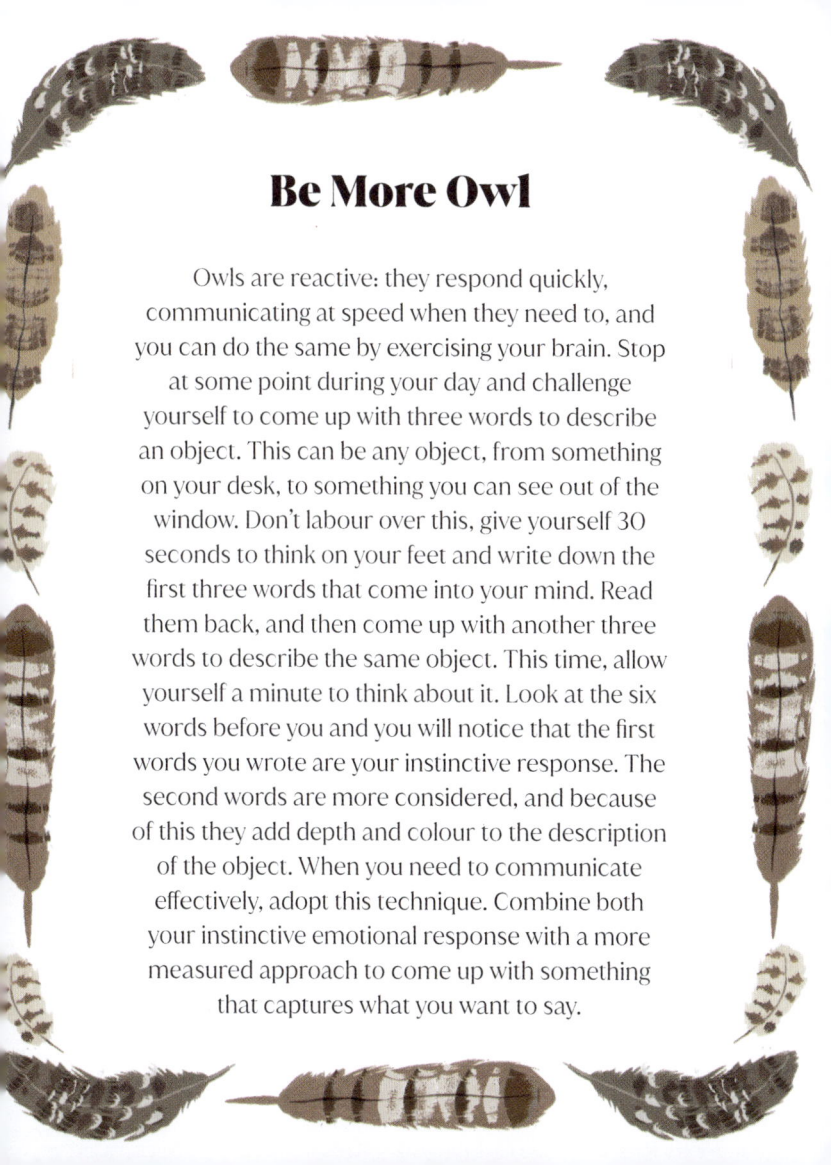

Owls are reactive: they respond quickly, communicating at speed when they need to, and you can do the same by exercising your brain. Stop at some point during your day and challenge yourself to come up with three words to describe an object. This can be any object, from something on your desk, to something you can see out of the window. Don't labour over this, give yourself 30 seconds to think on your feet and write down the first three words that come into your mind. Read them back, and then come up with another three words to describe the same object. This time, allow yourself a minute to think about it. Look at the six words before you and you will notice that the first words you wrote are your instinctive response. The second words are more considered, and because of this they add depth and colour to the description of the object. When you need to communicate effectively, adopt this technique. Combine both your instinctive emotional response with a more measured approach to come up with something that captures what you want to say.

Know Yourself

To speak your truth, you must first know and value yourself. We often take our gifts and talents for granted, when others can clearly see our potential. Once you accept and acknowledge your unique abilities and what makes you tick, you will be able to **find your voice** and make a mark on the world, just as the wise owl knows the skills and talents available to attract a mate, and truly thrive in the avian kingdom.

To help you get to know yourself better and embrace your special qualities, try this step-by-step approach.

Step One

Make a list of your talents and skills. Don't be shy – think about all of the things that you enjoy and do well.

Step Two

Make another list of all your positive qualities. Again, don't hold back with this. Think about all of the lovely compliments you have received from other people. You know in your heart what makes you special; it's about acknowledging this.

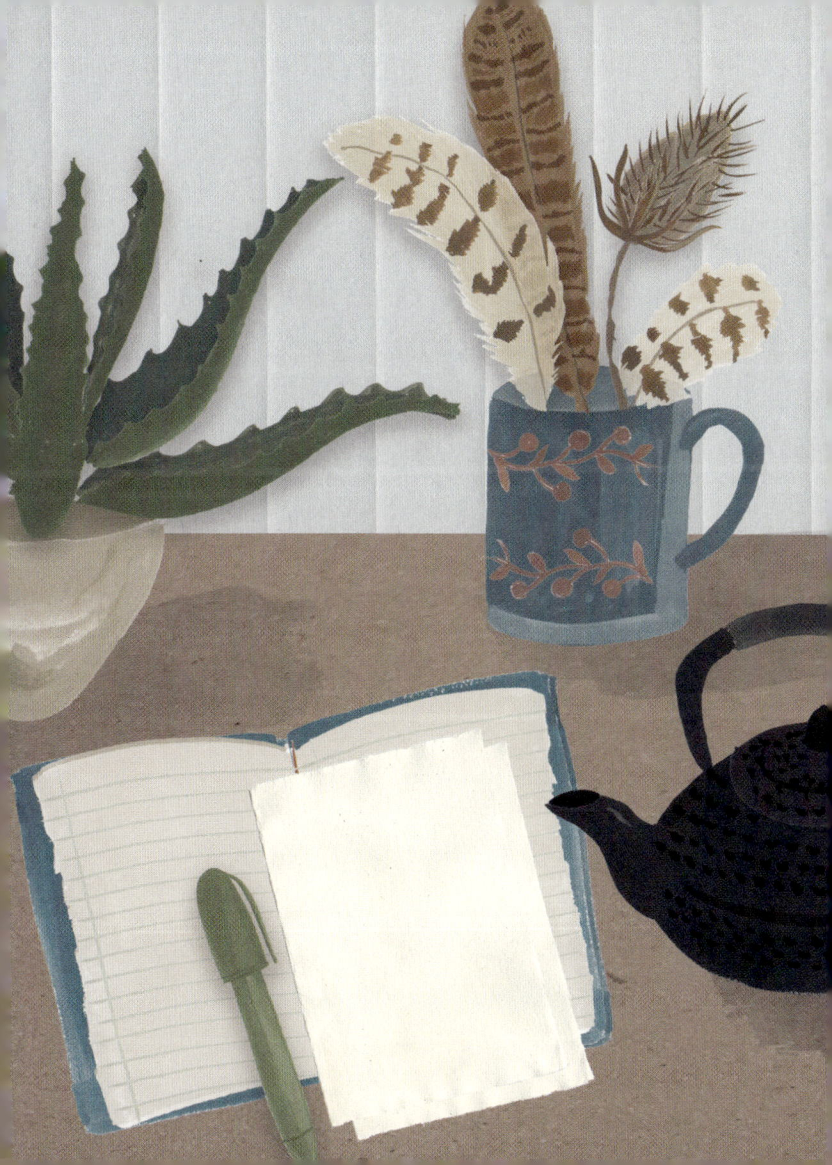

Step Three

Ask friends and family members for their help. What do they love about you? Even if you don't agree with their comments, add them to the list. This is about the wonderful things that others see in you.

Step Four

Spend some time reading through both lists. Accept that all of these things make you unique and let the truth of the words wash over you.

Step Five

Pin both lists up somewhere that you can see them and read them regularly. Remind yourself every day that you are amazing, and remember to add to the lists too, as you discover more positive traits and skills.

Be More Owl

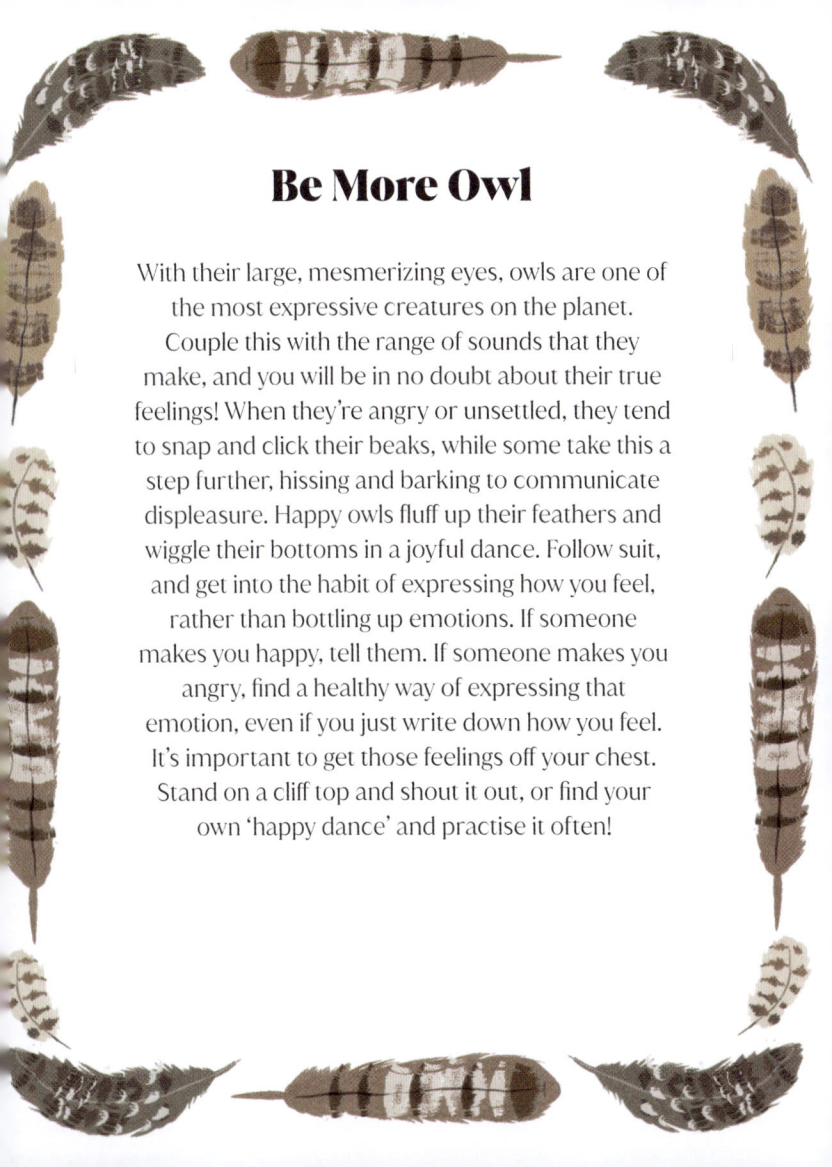

With their large, mesmerizing eyes, owls are one of the most expressive creatures on the planet. Couple this with the range of sounds that they make, and you will be in no doubt about their true feelings! When they're angry or unsettled, they tend to snap and click their beaks, while some take this a step further, hissing and barking to communicate displeasure. Happy owls fluff up their feathers and wiggle their bottoms in a joyful dance. Follow suit, and get into the habit of expressing how you feel, rather than bottling up emotions. If someone makes you happy, tell them. If someone makes you angry, find a healthy way of expressing that emotion, even if you just write down how you feel. It's important to get those feelings off your chest. Stand on a cliff top and shout it out, or find your own 'happy dance' and practise it often!

'Owl' Always Love You

Owls come in **ALL SHAPES AND SIZES**. Each one is a masterpiece, perfect in its own way. You too are a natural wonder made perfect as you are, but it can be hard to accept that. Learn to love yourself, feathers and all, with this simple technique to build confidence.

🪶 **Stand in front of a full-length mirror**, if you have one. If not, use a smaller mirror but make sure you can clearly see your face in the reflection.

🪶 **Gaze at the image**, and take in your beauty. This may feel odd at first, but stick with it.

🪶 **Smile** and notice how this one expression lifts your face and makes your eyes sparkle.

🪶 Instead of focusing on imperfections, **notice all the good things** about yourself. There is no one on the planet like you. You are a work of art.

🪶 Say **'I love myself'**, and repeat it loudly until you feel comfortable saying the words.

🪶 **Do this morning and night** every day, just like the owl who expresses its love at dusk and dawn.

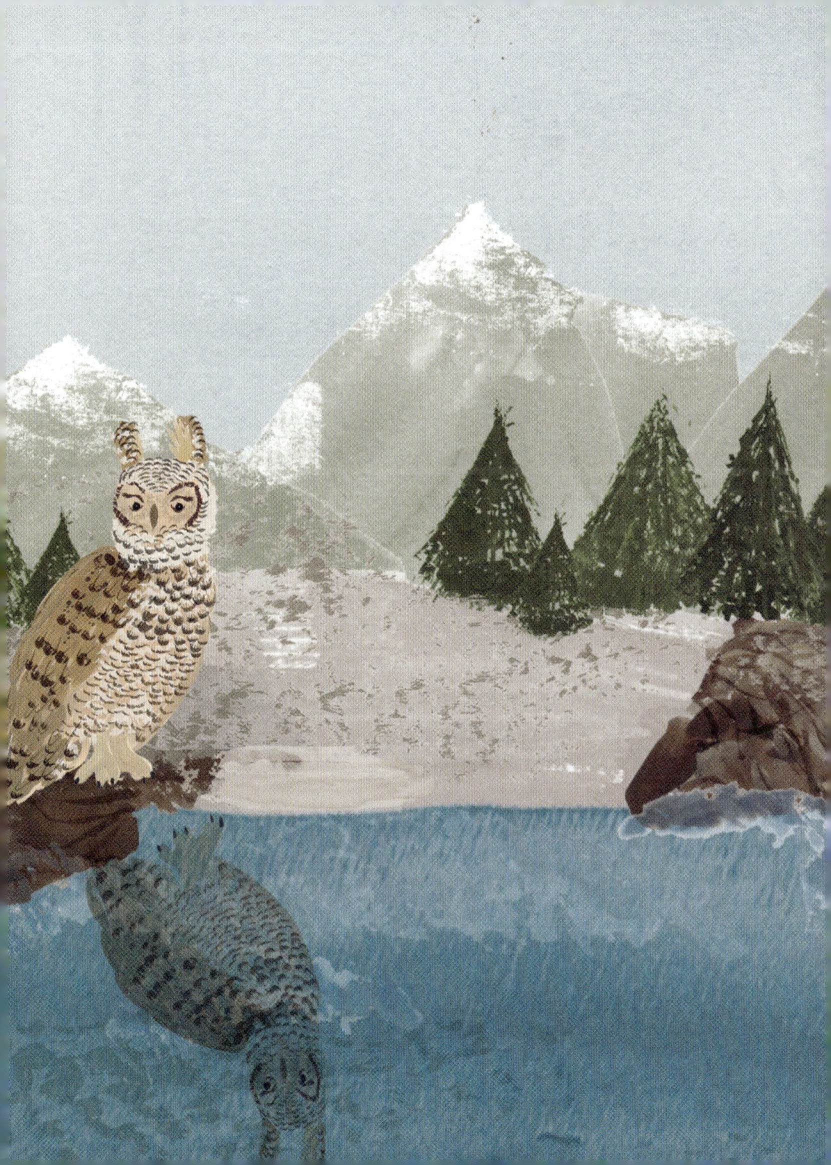

Owl Magic: Turquoise Charms

Turquoise is the stone of **COMMUNICATION**; it can help you find your voice and say what you mean with eloquence. Find a turquoise stone and a small picture of an owl. Invest in a velvet pouch and place the image and stone inside, or if you prefer, use a piece of dark material and bundle up the stone and picture inside, then tie it up with string or ribbon so that you have a little parcel. Keep this with you as a charm to help you express yourself effectively and creatively. Whenever you need to **speak your truth with confidence**, hold the charm bundle in your pocket and let the words flow.

OWL AFFIRMATIONS

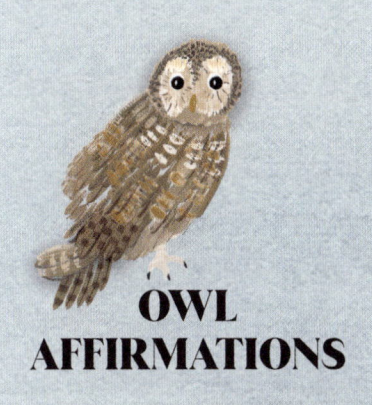

I am free to be who I want to be; I fly my own way.

Every day I express myself with ease,
clarity and confidence.

My creativity is an opportunity to show the world
who I truly am.

I allow my innate gifts to shine through in everything I do.
I am beautiful, just as I am.

There is no one in the world like me,
I am magical and unique.

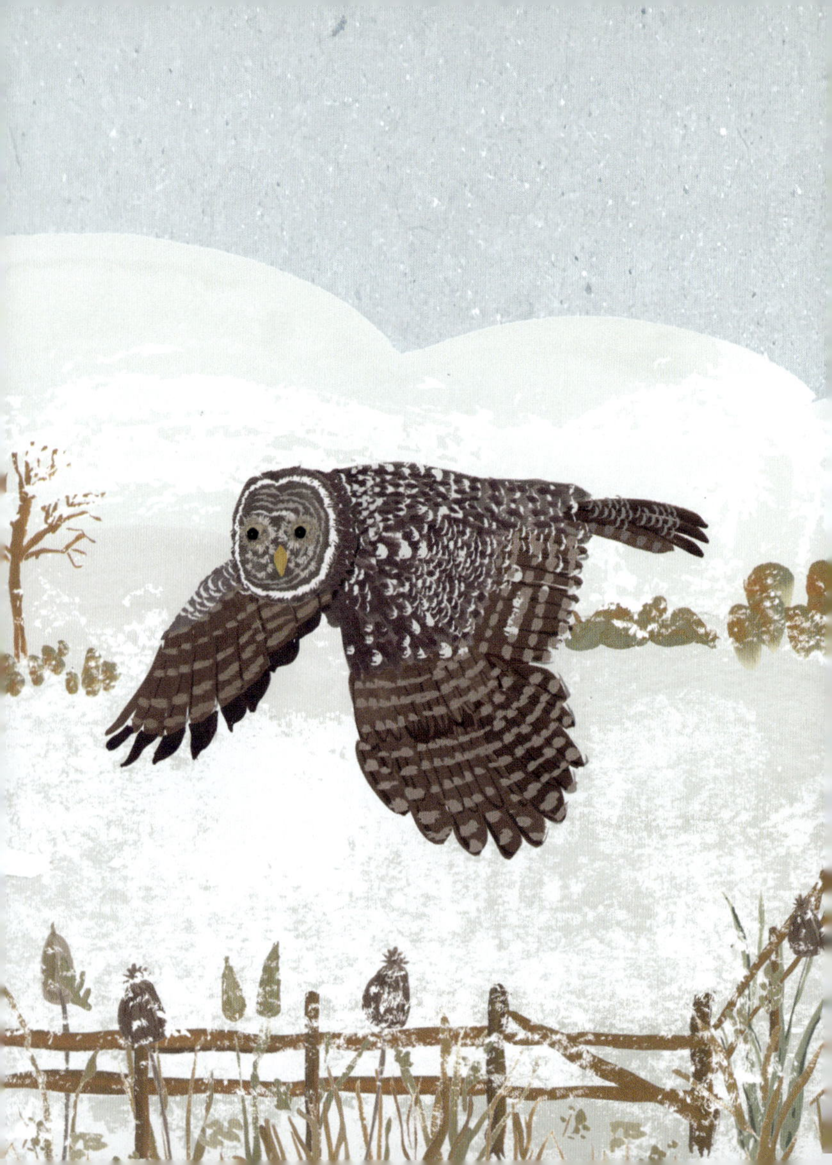

Chapter Three
Listen With Intent

'The owl is the wisest of all birds, because the more it sees, the less it talks.'

African proverb

It takes a special set of skills to secure a meal when dinner doesn't come served on a plate. Owls have plenty to call upon, but perhaps most important is their **keen hearing**. The great grey owl hears so well that it can listen out for the shuffling of small animals beneath the snow and know exactly where to strike. It isn't the only owl to rely on the power of sound. Barn owls hunting in the dead of night will **SWOOP** over open fields and rough terrain alike, and can pinpoint the tiniest mammals from a great height before diving to make their catch. Precision is the name of the game here, and it can only be achieved thanks to their superb hearing skills.

Of course, the owl is blessed in that department, for while their ears are cleverly obscured by a frame of feathers, they are exceptionally receptive. The thick ruff that sheaths each ear channels the sound in the right direction, giving each discerning owl a heads-up when there's anything of interest to be heard. **Worm in mid-squirm?** Easily snaffled, thanks to an updraft of sound. But there's more to this hearing lark than a discreet funnel of feathers.

The owl's flattened facial disc allows sound to be channelled in the right direction, and its ears are asymmetrical, with the left one being lower than the right, meaning that sounds hit them at a different time. This

STAGGERED SYMPHONY helps the bird pinpoint exactly where the noise is coming from and their ear drums, which are significantly bigger than most birds', transform the airborne waves into fluid vibrations. These tiny shivers travel through delicate hairs within the inner ear, allowing the owl to 'see' and 'sense' a bigger picture. **Voilà, dinner is served!**

But it's not only their natural talents that make owls such great listeners – they put in the hard work, too! Masters of motivation and focus, they know how to apply themselves to the task in hand. While it's easy to hear the whistling wind in the trees or a **'TWIT TWOO'** on the breeze, it takes real concentration to listen out for those tiny noises of the night. **Dedication is key.** Taking time to focus beyond the surface noise makes all the difference when you cannot see the light.

We could all learn from owls on this matter – truly listening, so that we not only hear people's words but their core meaning. Life is a rugged expanse of woodland with peaks, troughs and plenty beneath the surface, but to find those nuggets of joy that will sustain us, we need to fully engage with what's going on around us. We must learn to focus on the true meaning of each interaction, spoken or otherwise, and **LISTEN WITH ALL OF OUR SENSES.**

Be More Owl

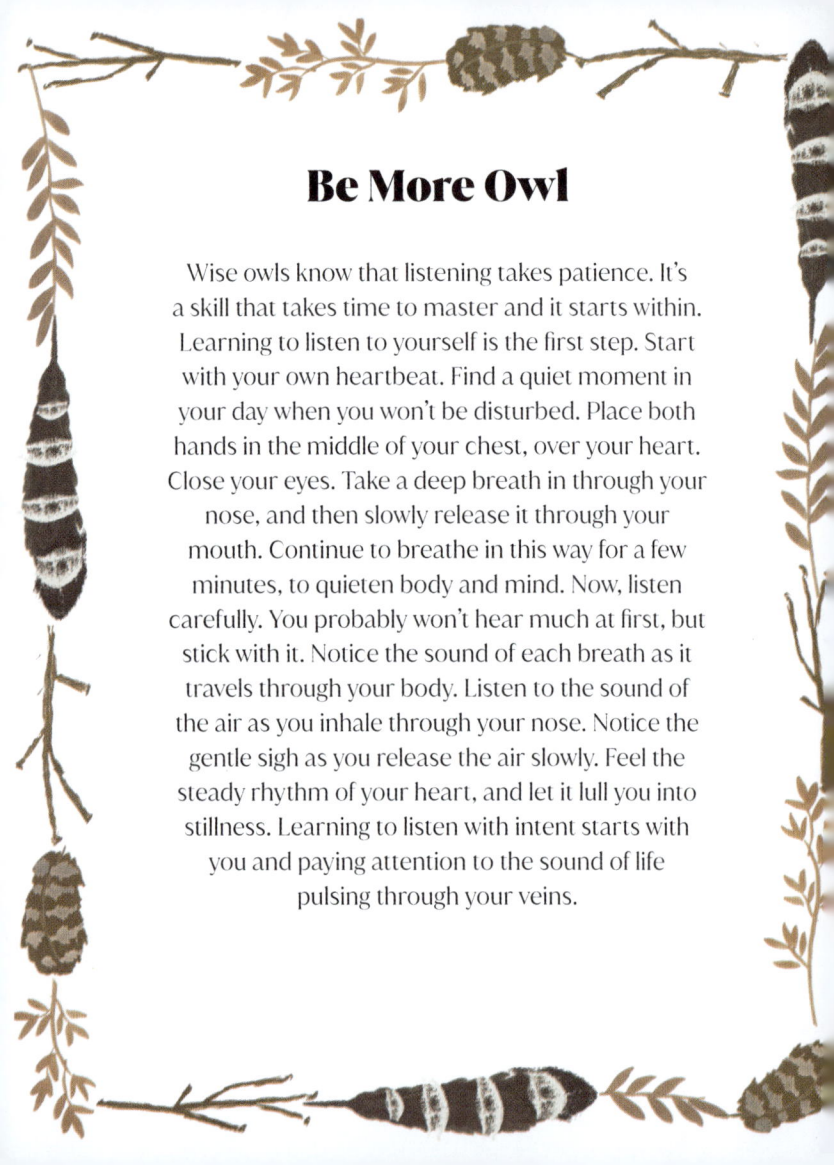

Wise owls know that listening takes patience. It's a skill that takes time to master and it starts within. Learning to listen to yourself is the first step. Start with your own heartbeat. Find a quiet moment in your day when you won't be disturbed. Place both hands in the middle of your chest, over your heart. Close your eyes. Take a deep breath in through your nose, and then slowly release it through your mouth. Continue to breathe in this way for a few minutes, to quieten body and mind. Now, listen carefully. You probably won't hear much at first, but stick with it. Notice the sound of each breath as it travels through your body. Listen to the sound of the air as you inhale through your nose. Notice the gentle sigh as you release the air slowly. Feel the steady rhythm of your heart, and let it lull you into stillness. Learning to listen with intent starts with you and paying attention to the sound of life pulsing through your veins.

Owl Spotlight

Barn Owl

One of the most widespread owl species, the barn owl can be found all over the world, except in polar and desert regions. The barn owl is medium sized with a pale face, chest and belly, and buff greyish upper parts. Its **long wings power it forward** and it has a short, squarish tail. Mostly nocturnal, this owl favours open fields and meadows to hunt, and will roost in cosy tree cavities and abandoned barns.

Mindful Walk

Owls take note of the environment. They engage with the world around them and navigate the landscape, making the most of every reverberation. You can do the same by learning to **listen to the sounds of your day** and connecting with each one.

A mindful walk is a great way to switch off and engage with your environment. You don't have to choose anywhere special to stroll; your regular route to work may seem boring, but you will see it in a new light when walking mindfully. That said, if you want to take the opportunity to **VISIT SOMEWHERE NEW**, then the experience will be enriched by engaging your senses.

Try this!

You will need:
Just yourself in some comfy shoes.

🌰 Set your intention before you leave home to fully connect with the landscape as you walk.

🌰 To begin, get into a rhythm with your walking. Listen to the sound of your footfalls, notice how it feels as your soles hit the ground and take note of the noise this makes.

🌿 Breathe deeply and take your time. Imagine that your ears are antennae and that they pick up every little noise embedded in the environment.

🌿 You may notice that there are layers of sound – from the obvious noises that can be heard above everything else, to the subtle sounds in the background.

🌿 Listen out for pinpricks of sound, from the distant tweet of a bird to the sound of leaves fluttering. You might not be able to see these things, but they are there and your ears can help you build a better picture.

🌿 If your concentration wavers, don't worry. Simply breathe and bring your attention back to the sound of your own body as you move, then expand your awareness outwards.

🌿 Enjoy your surroundings and breathe in the experience.

Be More Owl

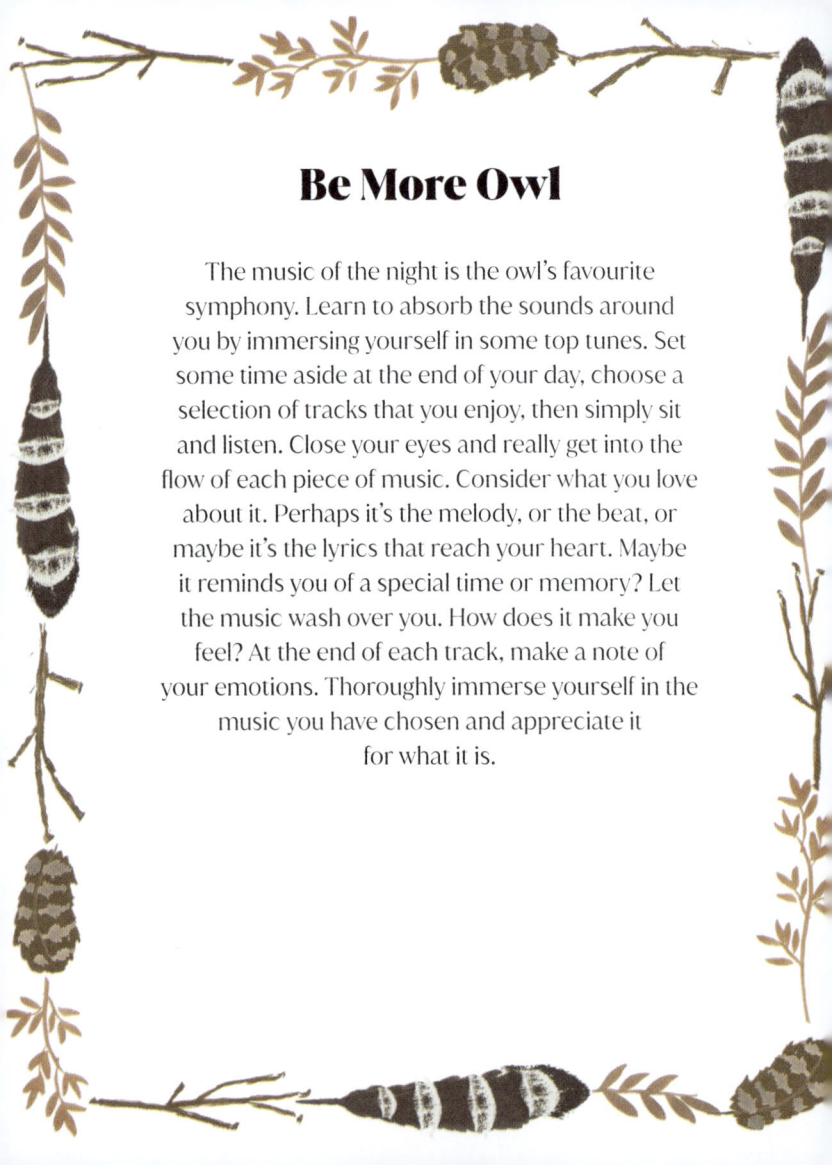

The music of the night is the owl's favourite symphony. Learn to absorb the sounds around you by immersing yourself in some top tunes. Set some time aside at the end of your day, choose a selection of tracks that you enjoy, then simply sit and listen. Close your eyes and really get into the flow of each piece of music. Consider what you love about it. Perhaps it's the melody, or the beat, or maybe it's the lyrics that reach your heart. Maybe it reminds you of a special time or memory? Let the music wash over you. How does it make you feel? At the end of each track, make a note of your emotions. Thoroughly immerse yourself in the music you have chosen and appreciate it for what it is.

Listen Without Words

You might think that listening comes naturally to you, but how much of your auditory sense do you use? We often think we are listening, when actually, **we're only taking in half of the information**. Think back to some of your recent interactions with others. How much can you remember? If you were put on the spot, could you say how the other person was really feeling?

LISTENING WITH INTENT means picking up the subtle clues that come with the words. Try these easy steps to improve your listening skills.

Step One

Breathe. Before you speak, take a long, deep breath in. As you listen, continue to breathe deeply. This one action will calm your mind and allow you to really 'hear' what is being said.

Step Two

Listen not only to the words that are being spoken, but also to how they are said. People place emphasis on certain words or phrases that are significant to them. Notice, too, the pauses before words; this usually means that what comes next will be important.

Step Three

Notice the tone of the person's voice and how it changes through the conversation. When someone is excited or happy, they tend to become more animated – words come faster and louder and the pitch of their voice may change. If someone is feeling relaxed, their tone will be lower. If there's frustration there, you will hear it in the staccato way they speak.

Step Four

Pay attention to your own emotions as you listen. You will react intuitively during a conversation, as natural feelings of empathy arise. If you feel sad, then it's likely that you're picking up on this emotion from the person you are with.

Step Five

As you hear each word, remember to engage your other senses. Notice the person's expression and how they move. Are they gesticulating a lot, or do they seem tense? If their body is laid-back, then it's likely they're relaxed. Take note of these details to get the full picture.

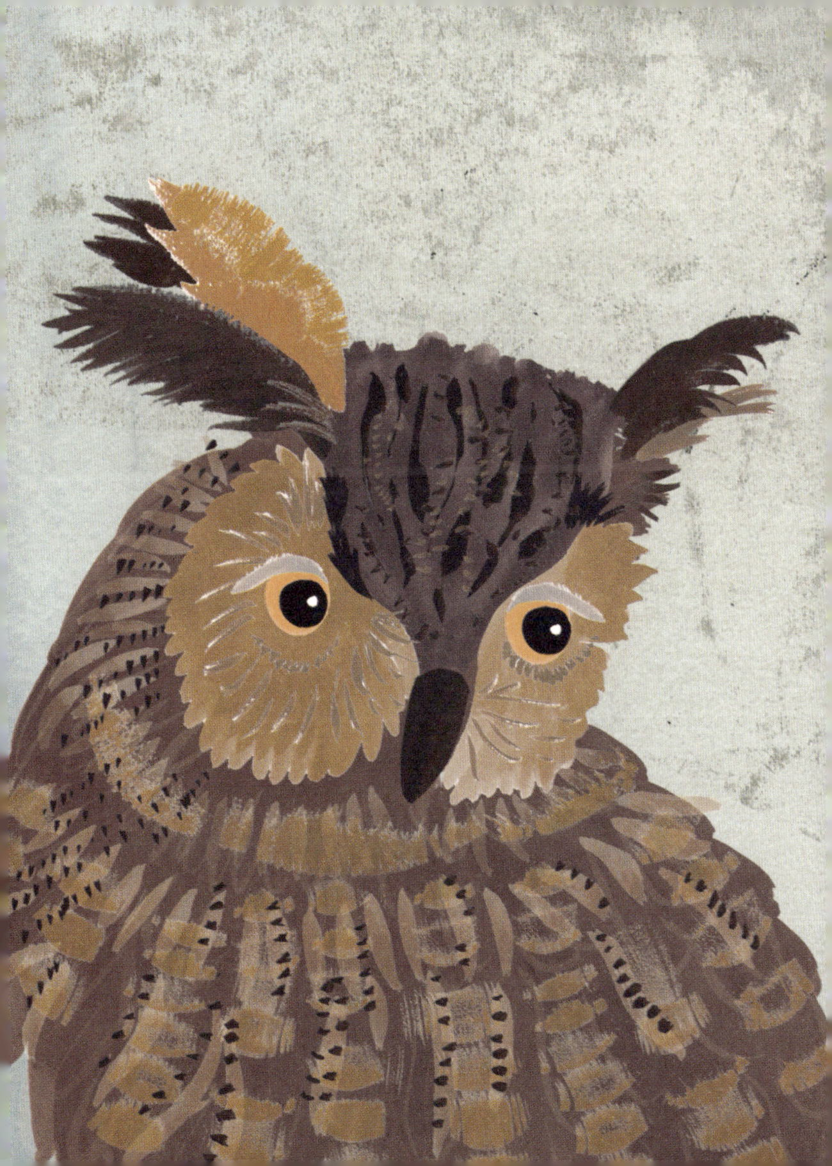

Be More Owl

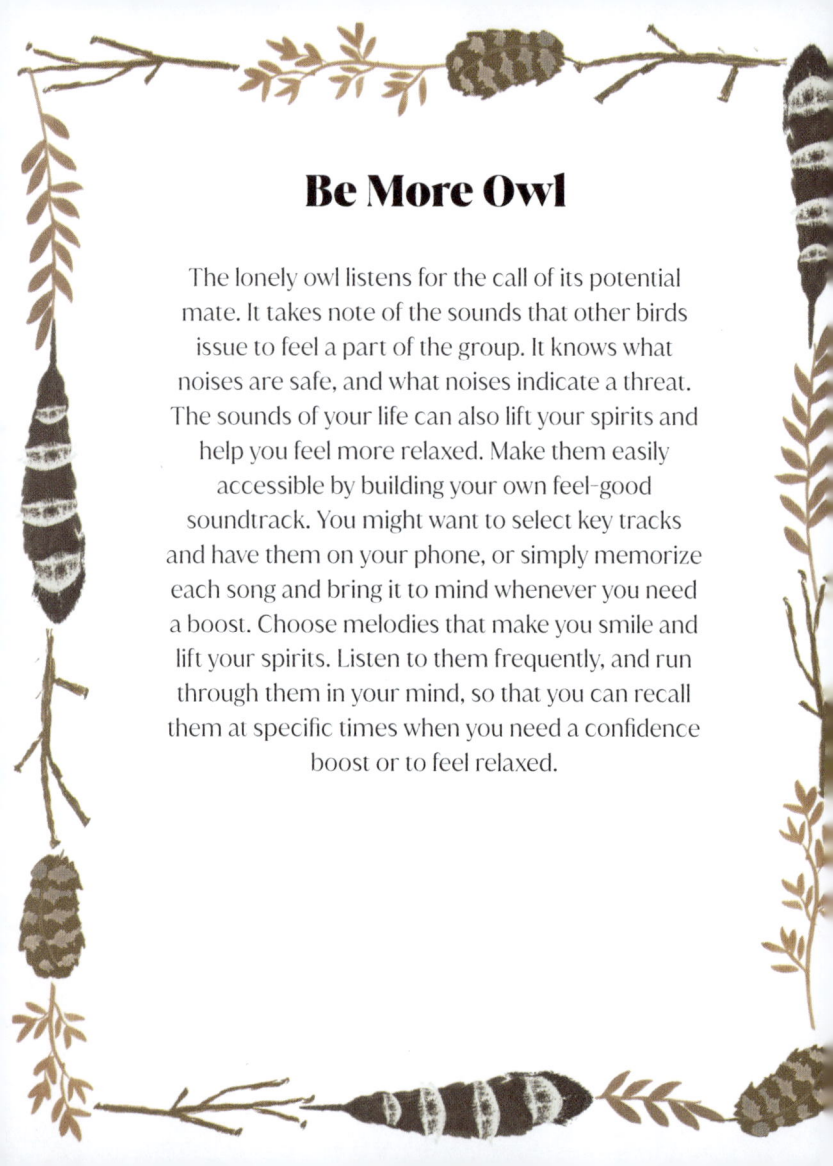

The lonely owl listens for the call of its potential mate. It takes note of the sounds that other birds issue to feel a part of the group. It knows what noises are safe, and what noises indicate a threat. The sounds of your life can also lift your spirits and help you feel more relaxed. Make them easily accessible by building your own feel-good soundtrack. You might want to select key tracks and have them on your phone, or simply memorize each song and bring it to mind whenever you need a boost. Choose melodies that make you smile and lift your spirits. Listen to them frequently, and run through them in your mind, so that you can recall them at specific times when you need a confidence boost or to feel relaxed.

Hear With Your Heart

It's easy to listen and hear what we want to hear. It's more difficult to understand what is truly being said, especially when emotions are involved. Owls are gifted with asymmetrical ears, which means that information in the form of sound waves is staggered, helping them to see what is hidden. Communication is a two-way process, but to really understand where someone is coming from, you need to put yourself in their shoes and hear with your heart. The following tips will help you do this.

🍂 **Take your time when listening.** Don't rush the other person; let them speak without interruption so that they have enough time to articulate how they feel.

🍂 **Don't rush to respond to what someone is saying.** Digest the words and give yourself time to understand the meaning behind them, then formulate a considered response.

🍂 **Be honest with the other person.** If there's something you don't understand, tell them. Be sure you comprehend their true meaning. We often misinterpret what people say because we have our own agenda, so before you jump to any conclusions first ask yourself, 'Am I hearing this correctly, or am I coloured by my own thoughts and feelings?'

🌱 **Try and put yourself in their shoes.** Think about where they are coming from, and how they might be feeling. Listening to the way they speak will give you clues to their emotional state.

🌱 **Hear with your heart** – slow things right down and allow your senses to guide you. To help with this, slow your breathing by taking longer, deeper breaths. Release any tension you might feel as you exhale.

🌱 **Imagine that your heart and mind open up** a little more with every breath and you're able to understand what is being said. As you inhale, picture your heart swelling with love; as you exhale, imagine that it expands, filling your entire chest. See your heart as an extended part of your auditory system, helping you to hear with love.

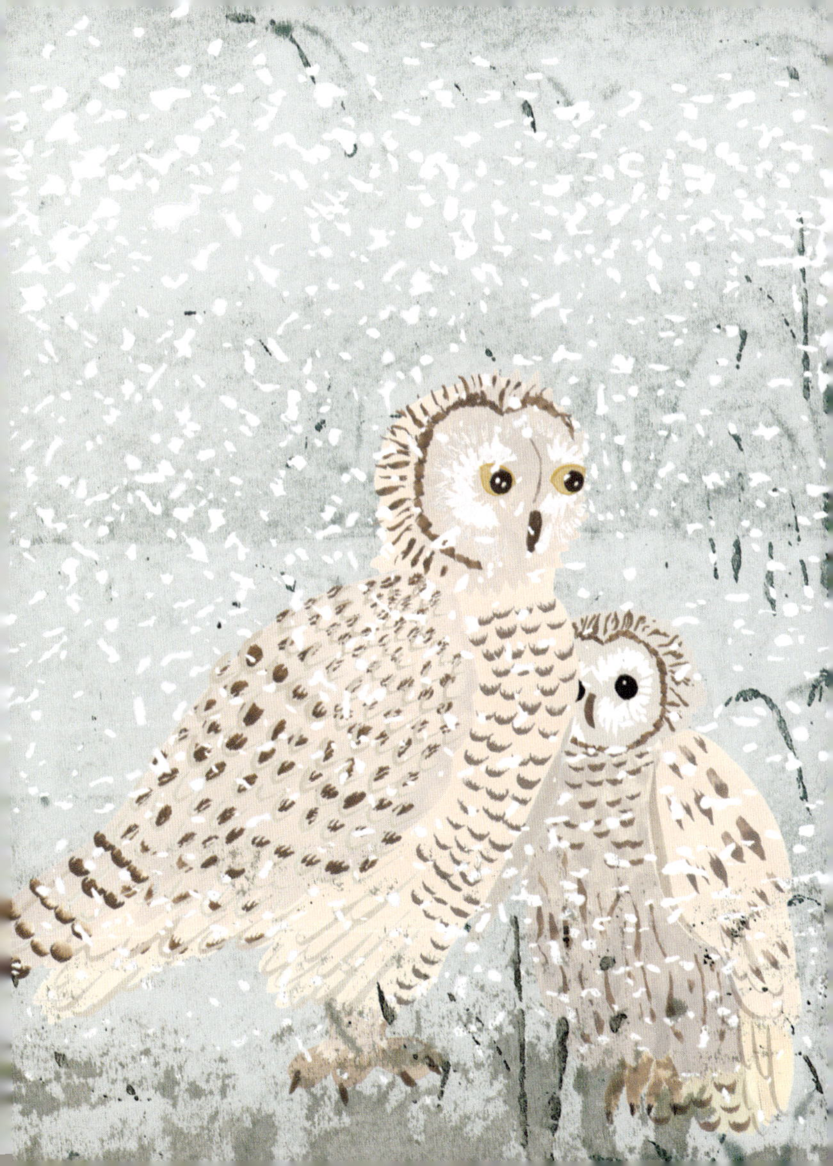

Owl Magic: Elemental Wind Chimes

Owls rely on the elements to help them navigate the landscape. They listen for **sounds carried along the breeze**, and this helps them build a more detailed picture of their environment. Open your ears and your heart and connect with the world around you, by harnessing the element of air. Invest in a wind chime that you can position near a window or door, and personalize it by adding a few extra decorations. Feathers are a brilliant addition as they are linked to both birds and the air; you might also want to add shells or beads. Use a length of string to thread on your new additions, then tie them to the main body of the chime so that they hang down. Take five minutes every day to sit near your chime and listen to the **GENTLE MELODY** it creates as it dances in the breeze.

OWL AFFIRMATIONS

The sounds of my environment lift me up
and help me feel like I belong.

I listen between the words, to the core truth
in every conversation.

Every day, I connect in new ways
with the world around me.

The melody of life enriches my world.

I focus my attention in each moment,
and stretch my senses to their fullest.

Listening to the landscape brings me infinite joy.

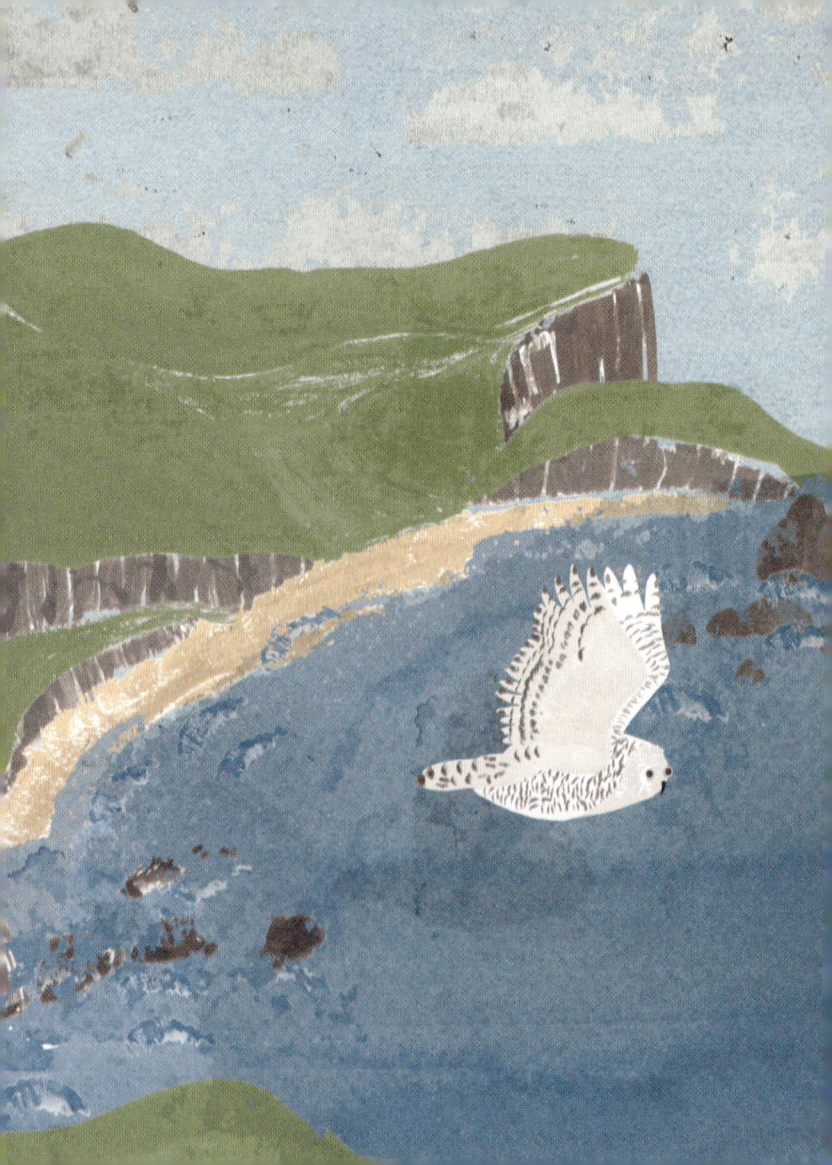

Chapter Four
See the Bigger Picture

'Owl
Wiser than can be
Seeing great at night
Flying quieter over the sea
Making hope shine bright.'

Unknown

If you're lucky enough to look into the eyes of an owl, you will see **a world of magic and wonderment**. It's easy to get lost in their gaze and many have wondered what wisdom lies behind these **BEAUTIFUL ORBS**. Indeed, owls' eyes are extraordinarily large, taking up half of the space in their skulls. They command attention, but like every aspect of an owl's make-up, they are there for a very good reason.

The owl's forward-facing eyes give it binocular vision, which is useful for hunting, and its retinas are uniquely adapted to help it to see in low light. Being observant is par for the course when you live in the shadows, but these birds have an uncanny ability to judge distance and see objects in three dimensions, which gives them the edge and elevates their status as one of the planet's top feathered predators. Add to this their discerning appearance, which comes from the forthright positioning of each eye, and you can see how they got their reputation for knowledge. Every owl worth its 'twit twoo' knows **the power of perspective** and how to look beyond the surface, for there is always something new to discover, be it a tasty morsel scurrying through the undergrowth or something more sinister highlighted by the moon's otherworldly glow. And having such large, all-encompassing windows with which to view the world, means **THEY DON'T MISS A TRICK.**

In spite of their wide-eyed appearance, owls don't have eyeballs like humans do. Instead, their eyes are tube-like in shape, and are held in place by a bony scaffolding. This keeps them rigid and steady so that they have pinpoint precision, especially under low-light conditions, but it does restrict movement. They can't move their eyes in their sockets like we can, so their field of vision is determined by how far they can turn their heads. To compensate for this, owls have **FILOPLUMES**; a smattering of tiny hairs around their beaks and feet which help them sense prey. Intricately fine and with a few short barbs at the end of each shaft, these hairs are concealed beneath the feathers, and provide useful information on a range of variables, from wind and air pressure to the movement of specific feathers when flying. Combine this with the bird's flexible neck, which allows them to view a wider expanse, and you have everything you need to get ahead in life, and **reach the front of the dinner queue**.

The neck is everything when it comes to viewpoint. Turning your head completely upside down might sound like an extreme sport to us, but to this bird, it's as natural as breathing. The **270-DEGREE ROTATION** of an owl's neck is as simple as a sidelong glance thanks to super-adaptable joints between the bones, which rotate in unison with a twisting spine. While this thought may have you seeking out a chiropractor, it's important to remember that **a flexible body equals a flexible mind**, and this is key to staying at the top of the food chain. Flexibility is an asset for humans too, helping us stay sharp, focused and ready for anything!

A **BIGGER PICTURE** is something that owls always seek; they know the value of perspective in every situation. Couple this with innate patience, which allows them to watch events unfold under the cover of night, and you have a winning combination. We may not be gifted with the same elasticity and night vision, but we can learn to be more objective in our approach to life's challenges. We can be open in body and mind, flexible in attitude and develop an on-the-fly approach to whatever comes our way, just by **broadening our viewpoint**.

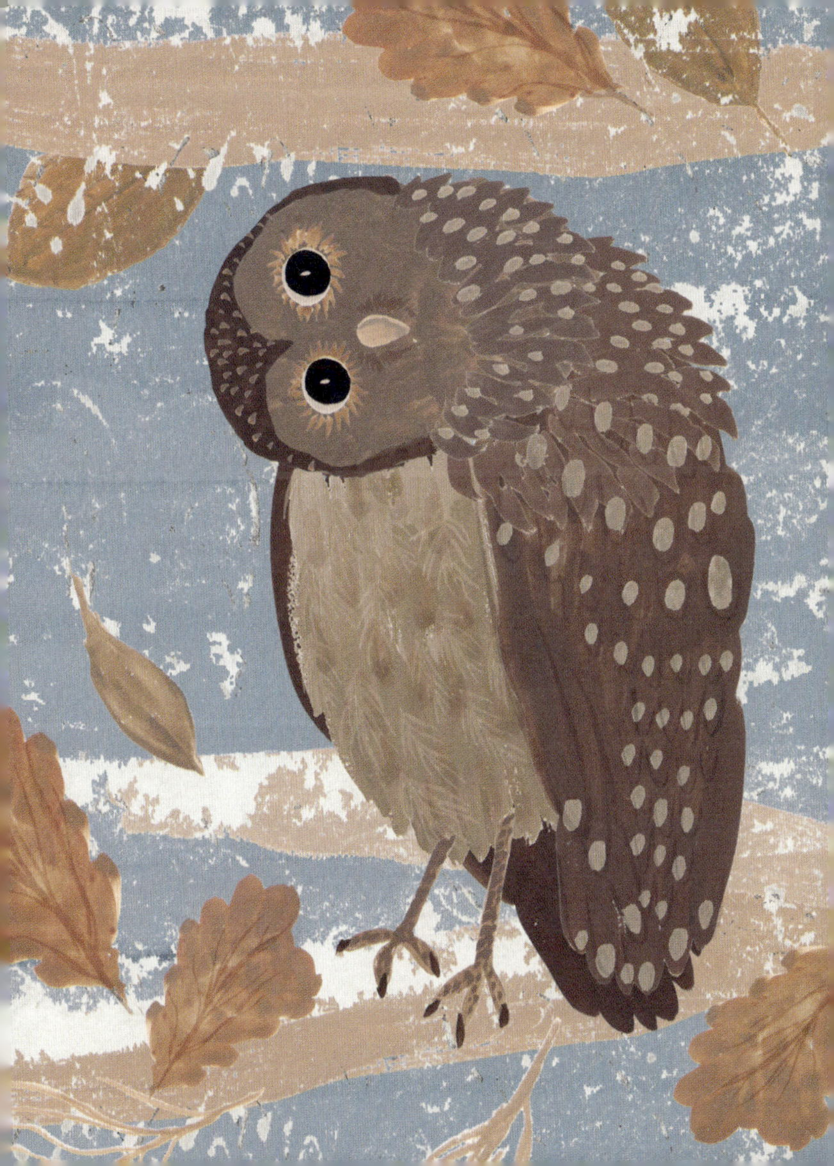

Be More Owl

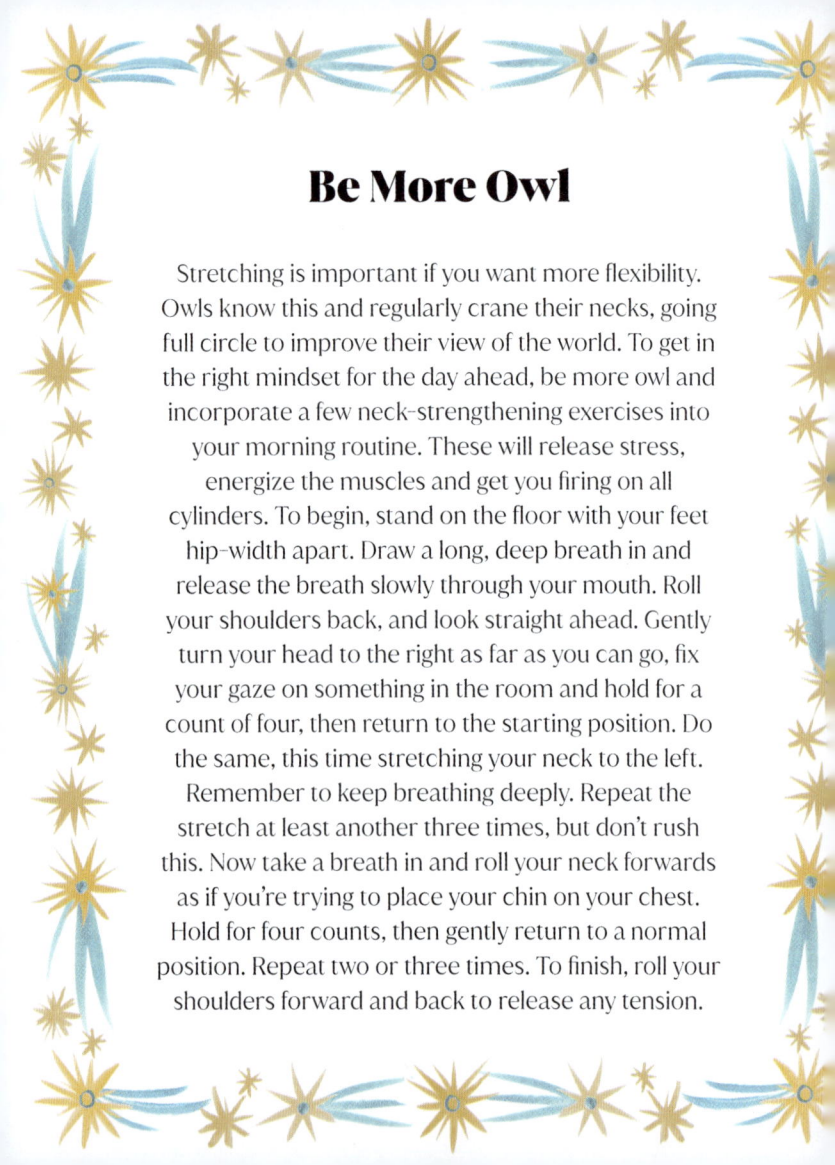

Stretching is important if you want more flexibility. Owls know this and regularly crane their necks, going full circle to improve their view of the world. To get in the right mindset for the day ahead, be more owl and incorporate a few neck-strengthening exercises into your morning routine. These will release stress, energize the muscles and get you firing on all cylinders. To begin, stand on the floor with your feet hip-width apart. Draw a long, deep breath in and release the breath slowly through your mouth. Roll your shoulders back, and look straight ahead. Gently turn your head to the right as far as you can go, fix your gaze on something in the room and hold for a count of four, then return to the starting position. Do the same, this time stretching your neck to the left. Remember to keep breathing deeply. Repeat the stretch at least another three times, but don't rush this. Now take a breath in and roll your neck forwards as if you're trying to place your chin on your chest. Hold for four counts, then gently return to a normal position. Repeat two or three times. To finish, roll your shoulders forward and back to release any tension.

See the Bigger Picture

Look Beyond the Veil

Our feathered friends know that there is magic in the mystery of night, and that beneath the **blanket of darkness**, many treasures can be found. They are prepared to look a little deeper and longer than most, in their bid to unveil these foodie treats. No wonder they're so wise! We can learn much from this attitude, by taking our time and being mindful of the world around us.

Try this!

You will need:
A place to sit where you have a view of the outside world.

🌿 Make sure you are comfortable, as you will be here a while. Get yourself into a position from where you can clearly see the outside world.

🌿 Slow your breathing right down by focusing on the journey of each breath.

🌿 As you inhale, hold on to the breath in your chest for a little longer than usual, then release it slowly.

🌿 Look at the outside view. What can you see?

See the Bigger Picture

🍂 Take in the overall view, then begin to focus on the different elements. Perhaps you notice a specific tree. Take a minute to home in and really look at all aspects of the tree: its size and shape, the colour, the pattern of the leaves on the branches and how they move in the breeze.

🍂 If your attention wavers from the object you have chosen, don't worry, just breathe and bring your gaze back to it.

🍂 When you're ready, move on to something else and take the same approach, taking time and care to really 'see' the object in your field of vision. You might find that you notice something you haven't before, or that it conjures up emotions or triggers memories.

🍂 Enjoy watching the world outside, taking in the view and noticing all of the little treasures that might normally escape you.

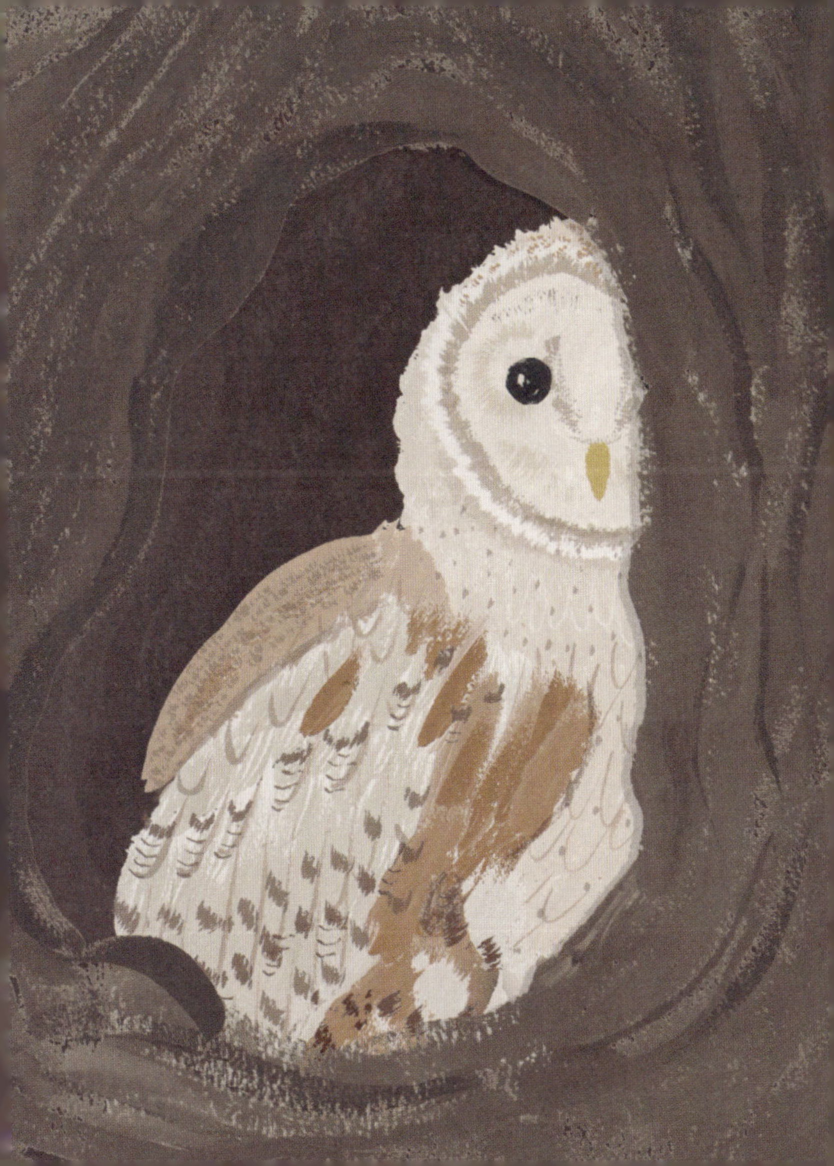

Be More Owl

Get into the habit of looking at things from a different perspective, like the owl who knows there's more than one way to view the world. Find a picture that you like and that you're familiar with – this may be a favourite portrait or just a sketch in a book that appeals to you. Now turn it upside down and look at it from a different angle. What do you see? Do you notice anything different? Perhaps the colours jump out at you or the lines remind you of something that you hadn't thought of before. Be creative as you gaze at it from a new angle. Imagine that the picture carries on, further than you can see, and let your mind wander. Allow your imagination to take over and have fun with this. Practising this exercise will help you view things more creatively.

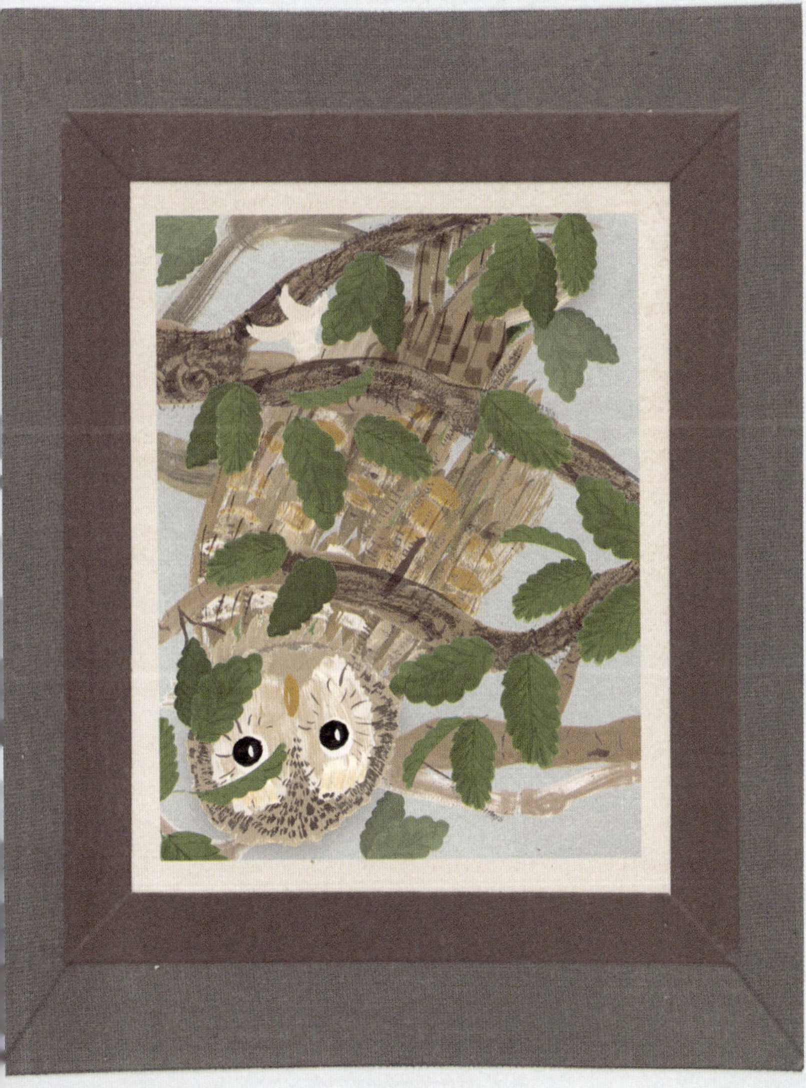

Practise Patience

One reason owls are such adept hunters is their innate patience. They **take their time** to assess the view, gathering all the information they need to plan their attack. This precise approach increases their chances of success, and you can adopt the same tactic when dealing with others. Instead of jumping the gun in challenging situations, take your time and **PRACTISE PATIENCE** in all your dealings with others.

Step One

Pause and take a deep breath. When you're face to face with a colleague, friend or partner and feel under threat, or that you might want to lash out with words, take a breath and, as you do, imagine falling back into yourself. Place your attention on the back of your body, relax and breathe.

Step Two

Once you've taken a breath, take a physical step back. A little distance relieves the tension and allows you both space to think.

Step Three

Remind yourself that you may only be seeing half of the picture. For example, if a colleague is upset about a work issue and has confronted you, it may be that they have other things going on in their life which have aggravated the situation. Just as you may have things going on, which are affecting the way you react.

Step Four

Bring to mind a happy situation. Consider a time when you felt more relaxed and recreate it in your mind. This will alleviate the pressure you currently feel and help you practise patience and kindness in your approach.

Step Five

Breathe. The most important thing you can do to develop patience is to remember to breathe and to do this slowly. This simple function clears your mind and allows you to relax and assess what is really going on so that you can act from a place of calm.

Be More Owl

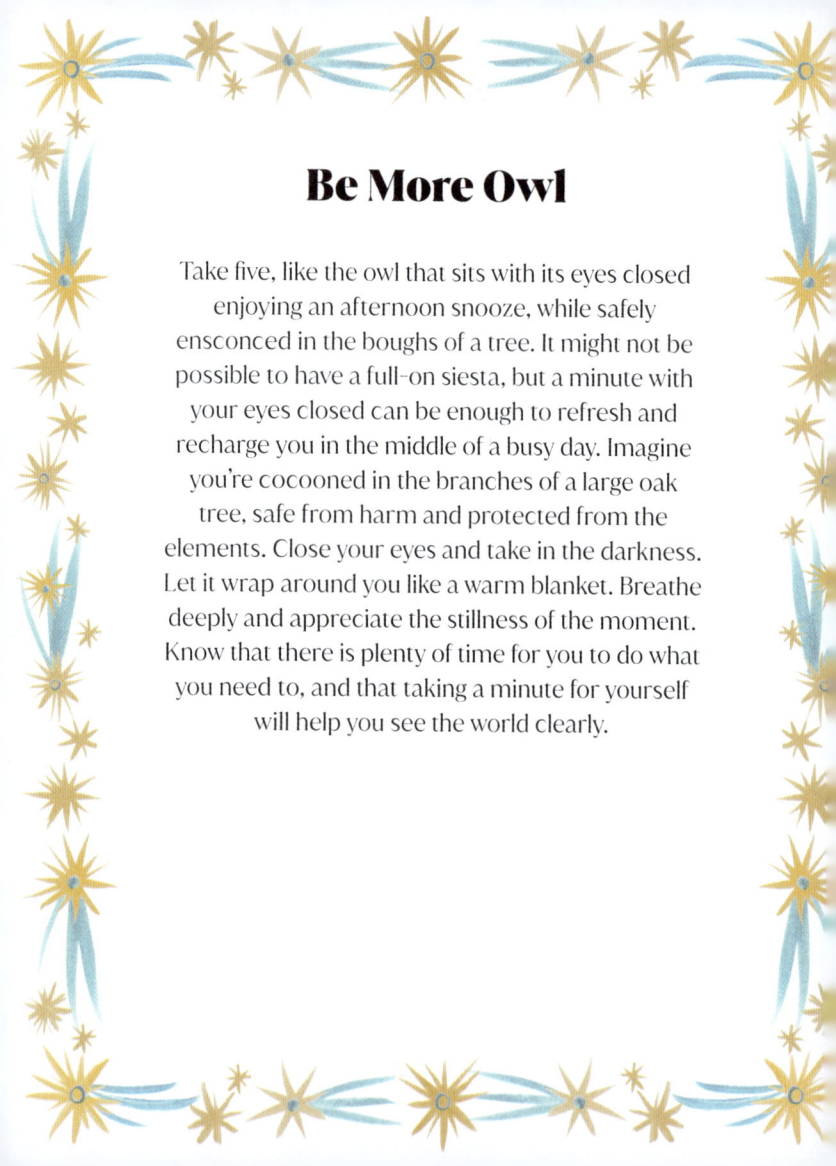

Take five, like the owl that sits with its eyes closed enjoying an afternoon snooze, while safely ensconced in the boughs of a tree. It might not be possible to have a full-on siesta, but a minute with your eyes closed can be enough to refresh and recharge you in the middle of a busy day. Imagine you're cocooned in the branches of a large oak tree, safe from harm and protected from the elements. Close your eyes and take in the darkness. Let it wrap around you like a warm blanket. Breathe deeply and appreciate the stillness of the moment. Know that there is plenty of time for you to do what you need to, and that taking a minute for yourself will help you see the world clearly.

See the Bigger Picture

Owl Spotlight

Little Owl

Although it is mainly nocturnal, the little owl can be seen roosting during the day. Its **tiny stature**, around 22cm (8½in) tall, is the reason for its name, but this dainty bird should not be underestimated. It can move at speed, with a rapid wingbeat and **BOUNCING FLIGHT**. The little owl has mottled brown and cream feathers, and it is found in a range of habitats across Europe, from farmland and woodland fringes to orchards and copses.

Stretch Your Routine

If you favour routine, make a point of shaking things up from time to time. Wise owls adapt and react, rather than doing the same thing every day. They may have their regular hunting grounds, but that doesn't mean they always take the same approach. Find a way to stretch yourself by introducing moments of spontaneity into your schedule.

🌿 **Take a different route to work than your usual commute.** If this isn't possible, shake things up by grabbing your morning brew from somewhere new.

🌿 **Wear something that you wouldn't normally.** This doesn't have to be something extravagant: choosing a different hair accessory, coat or bag will have an effect on your mood and make you feel renewed.

🌿 **Go for a walk and choose a new location or route.** Keep your mind open as you stroll and take in the vista with fresh eyes.

See the Bigger Picture

🌿 **Listen to something you wouldn't normally choose.** For example, try a different style of music or artist, or tune into a podcast or radio show that you've never listened to before. Open your mind and be flexible.

🌿 **Take up a new hobby.** This doesn't have to be anything dramatic. It can be something that you try at home if you don't feel brave enough to venture out to a new club or venue. Challenge yourself by doing something you wouldn't normally do.

Owl Magic: Dandelion Dreams

Owls are linked to the element of air; being able to fly helps them move with ease and grace from one place to another. Use the air's magic to help you be more flexible in your approach to the ups and downs of life and how you envision the future. Take the fluffy, feathery head of a seeded dandelion and hold it in both hands. Imagine that this delicate flower represents your hopes and dreams for the future. Stand outside on a windy day, cup the dandelion head in both hands and spin around. Take a deep breath and release the tufts into the wind. Say:

'Into the air, my hopes and dreams, fly free and return to me, as it is meant to be.'

Watch as the fluffy seeds are carried away by the breeze. Know that whatever life brings will be right for you, and that you have the flexibility of air at your fingertips.

OWL AFFIRMATIONS

I fly upon the breeze, and go with life's ebbs and flows.

The vista opens up to me in new ways;
I am able to see beyond the surface.

My body and mind are flexible in everything I do.

There is no need to rush, I take my time
and practise patience and kindness.

Every day is an opportunity to see
and appreciate something new.

My mind is open to new adventures.

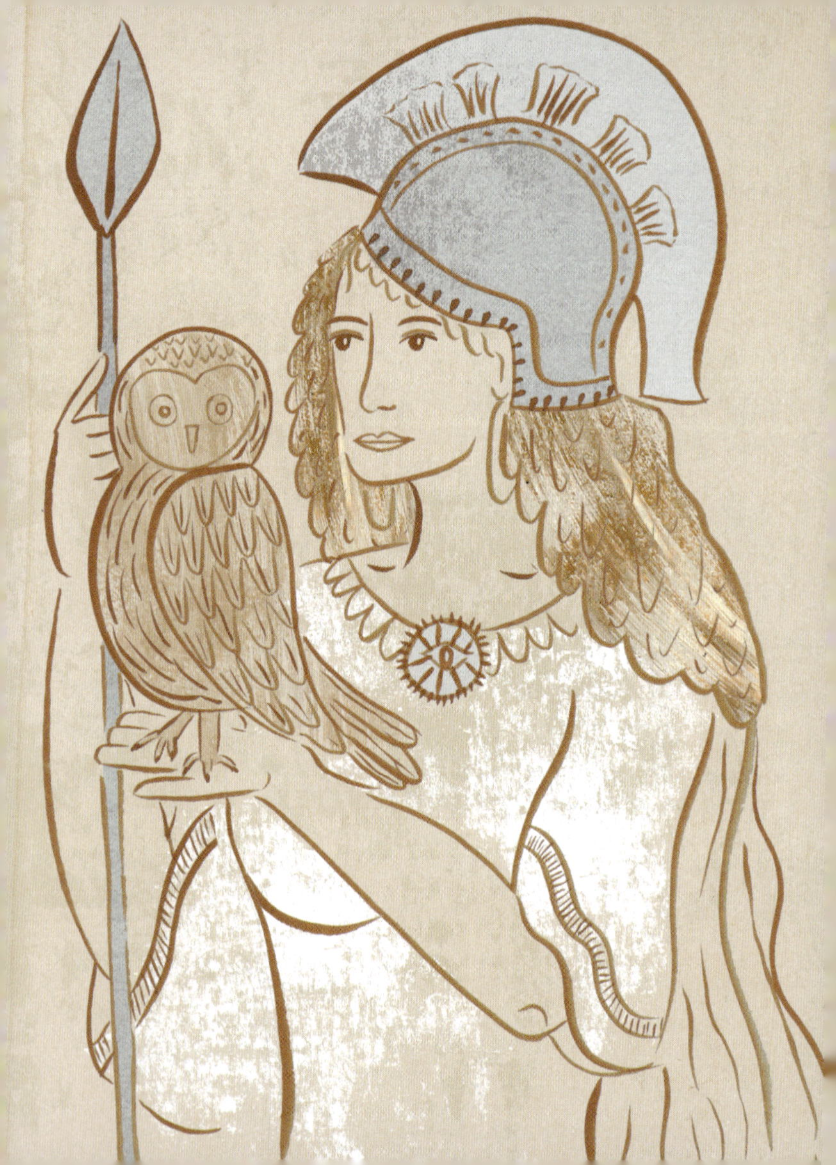

Chapter Five
Let Intuition Be Your Guide

'Owls remind us that wisdom comes from observing in silence.'

Unknown

If you've ever been face to face with an owl, you'll have felt the weight of its stare. Their **large, discerning eyes** appear all-knowing, as if seeing straight into your soul. It's easy to see why the ancients revered this bird. Its unique appearance, coupled with an **AURA OF MYSTERY**, was enough to leave the harshest critic spellbound. The fact that these birds could navigate the night with such skill added to their reputation, giving them an air of authority.

Belief in the owl's wisdom has often been coupled with a perceived connection to the otherworldly. Owls were the perfect heavenly consorts: **companions to the gods**, they could scale great heights, delivering a deathly cry and appearing as an omen to sleeping mortals. Rarely seen in daylight hours, their secretive nature linked them to the esoteric. After all, they were mostly invisible, able to evade discovery and melt seamlessly in their surroundings, which was seen as a gift from the gods.

Owls have cropped up in folklore around the world, where they favoured some deities over others. The Greek goddess **ATHENA** was the perfect example of the owl's friend. Associated with wisdom, knowledge and warfare, Athena had her wits about her and her trusty little owl perched upon her shoulder to whisper the secrets of the universe into her ear. Patron of the city of Athens, Athena was one of the Olympian Triad, ruling with Zeus and Apollo.

Her importance is reflected in the many relics containing her image, where she was often depicted with her owl close by. Being both a **SPIRITUAL GUIDE** and an advisor to the goddess, the owl was revered and protected, particularly within the Acropolis walls in Athens. Indeed, the city adopted this bird as a symbol of status and wisdom. Who better to watch over such a seat of power than the owl, with its keen, intuitive ways?

Athena's Roman counterpart, Minerva, was also a fan of this wise bird. The famous philosopher GWF Hegel once wrote, **'The owl of Minerva takes flight only at dusk'**, meaning, 'life can only be understood in retrospect'. Like Athena, Minerva was a military whizz known for her skills in battle strategy. She had governance of the Roman coin, commerce and industry and her wisdom was renowned throughout the land. No doubt the owl's insight gave her the edge when dealing with state affairs!

She wasn't the only one to benefit from this bird's savvy ways. The Slavic god of thunder and war, Perun, was also under its cosmic influence. Owls would follow in the wake of his storms, appearing as ghostly apparitions of the night. Lakshmi, the Indian goddess of **wealth and good fortune**, was depicted in the company of a white owl, making it an auspicious omen to many, while the Hopi Indians believed that the burrowing owl was their god of the dead. The creature's ability to traverse underground passages made it synonymous with the earth, and it was known as **'the watcher of the dark'**.

Throughout the world, the owl is recognized as an intuitive icon, offering **CLEAR VISION IN THE DARKNESS** and understanding with its insightful perceptions. It represents the unseen, a hidden world not unlike the subconscious mind, where clues can be found and true knowledge abounds. We too have access to this realm, by utilizing our psychic senses and **trusting our emotions**. If we can learn to read a situation and go beyond the superficial, we can easily gain the advantage and be more owl in our approach to life.

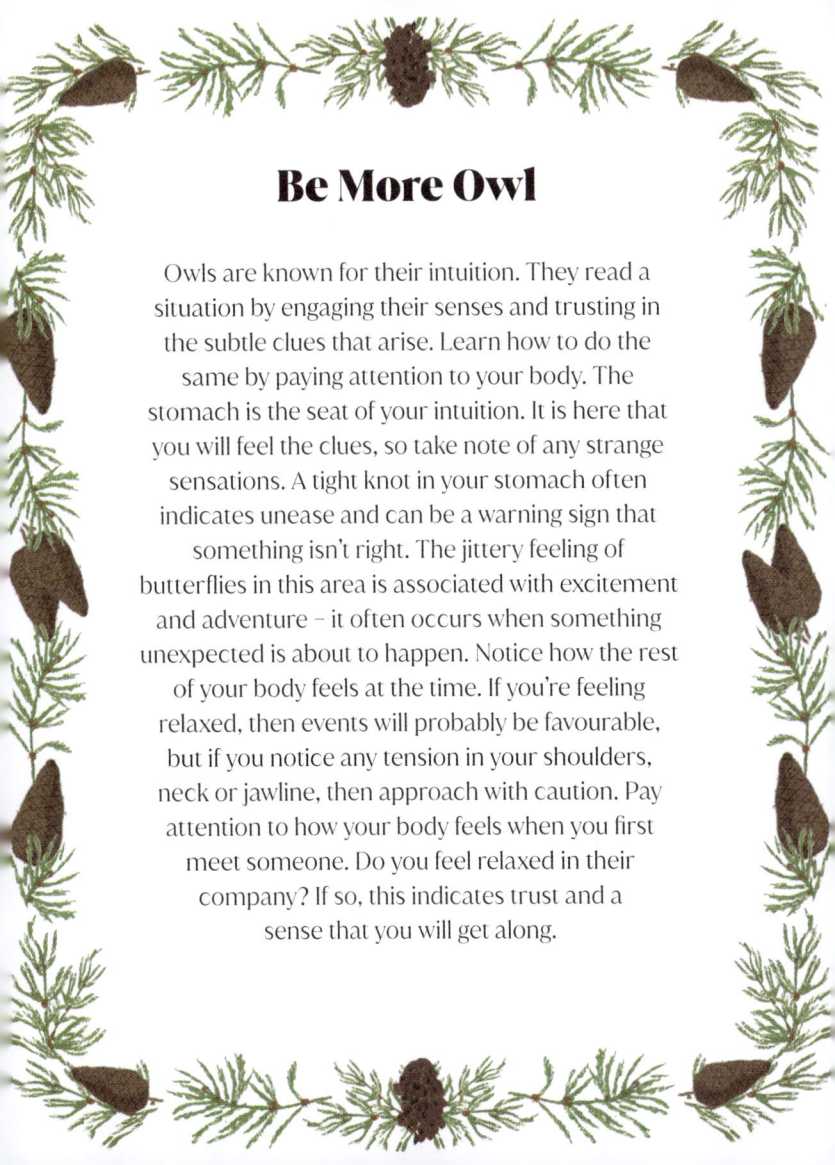

Be More Owl

Owls are known for their intuition. They read a situation by engaging their senses and trusting in the subtle clues that arise. Learn how to do the same by paying attention to your body. The stomach is the seat of your intuition. It is here that you will feel the clues, so take note of any strange sensations. A tight knot in your stomach often indicates unease and can be a warning sign that something isn't right. The jittery feeling of butterflies in this area is associated with excitement and adventure – it often occurs when something unexpected is about to happen. Notice how the rest of your body feels at the time. If you're feeling relaxed, then events will probably be favourable, but if you notice any tension in your shoulders, neck or jawline, then approach with caution. Pay attention to how your body feels when you first meet someone. Do you feel relaxed in their company? If so, this indicates trust and a sense that you will get along.

Meditate On It

Owls know the value of a quiet moment of contemplation. Whether they're taking five in a cosy corner or watching the world from on high, these perceptive birds know that **psychic insights come when you zone out**.

Meditation is a skill that can help you tap into your intuition. When you shut out the world and quieten your mind, you allow space for your **SUBCONSCIOUS MIND** to surface. It is in this state that you're likely to receive insights and visions that will help you deal with everyday situations.

Try this!

You will need:
A quiet space…

🌿 Find a space where you won't be disturbed and make yourself comfortable. If you can, settle down on the floor, and sit with your back supported by cushions or the wall.

🌿 Roll your shoulders back, and soften your chest.

🌿 Close your eyes and focus on your breathing. Follow the trail of the breath as you take in the air. Count slowly as you inhale, then slowly release the breath through your mouth.

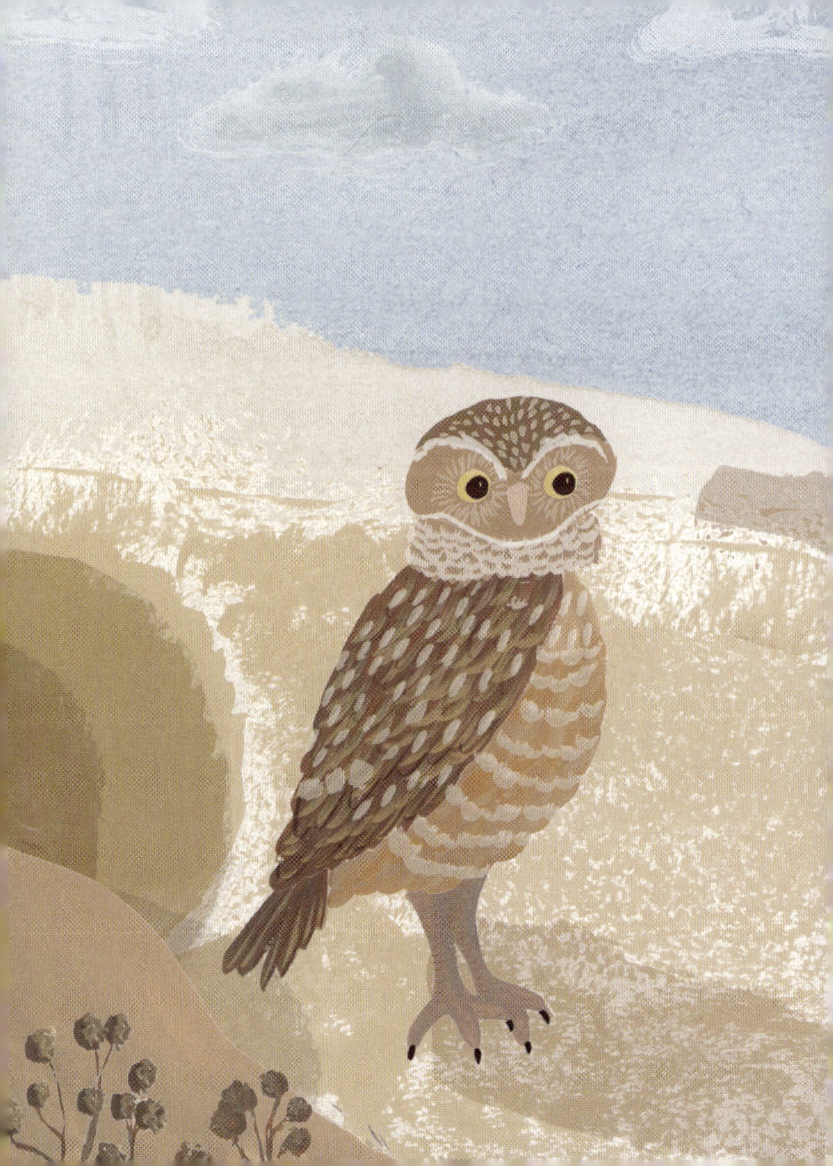

- Continue to breathe in this way, taking your time.

- In your mind, imagine you're face to face with an owl. This can be any owl of your choosing.

- Hold the owl's gaze, and look deeply into its eyes.

- Imagine that its eyes are getting bigger and darker. Feel yourself falling into their stare.

- Focus your mind, and let the eyes be the only thing you see. If your attention wavers, bring it back to the eyes and continue to breathe deeply.

- You may notice that the picture changes, or that you see images or patterns reflected in the surface of the eyes. You may feel emotions, too. Let these thoughts and feelings arise and acknowledge them, then let them go.

- When you're ready, imagine stepping back from the owl.

- Let the image of the bird fade away and open your eyes.

- Give your body a gentle stretch or shake.

- Make a note of any thoughts or feelings that surfaced during the meditation. These could be insightful clues or messages that make sense to you in the future.

- Practise this exercise regularly to boost your intuition.

Be More Owl

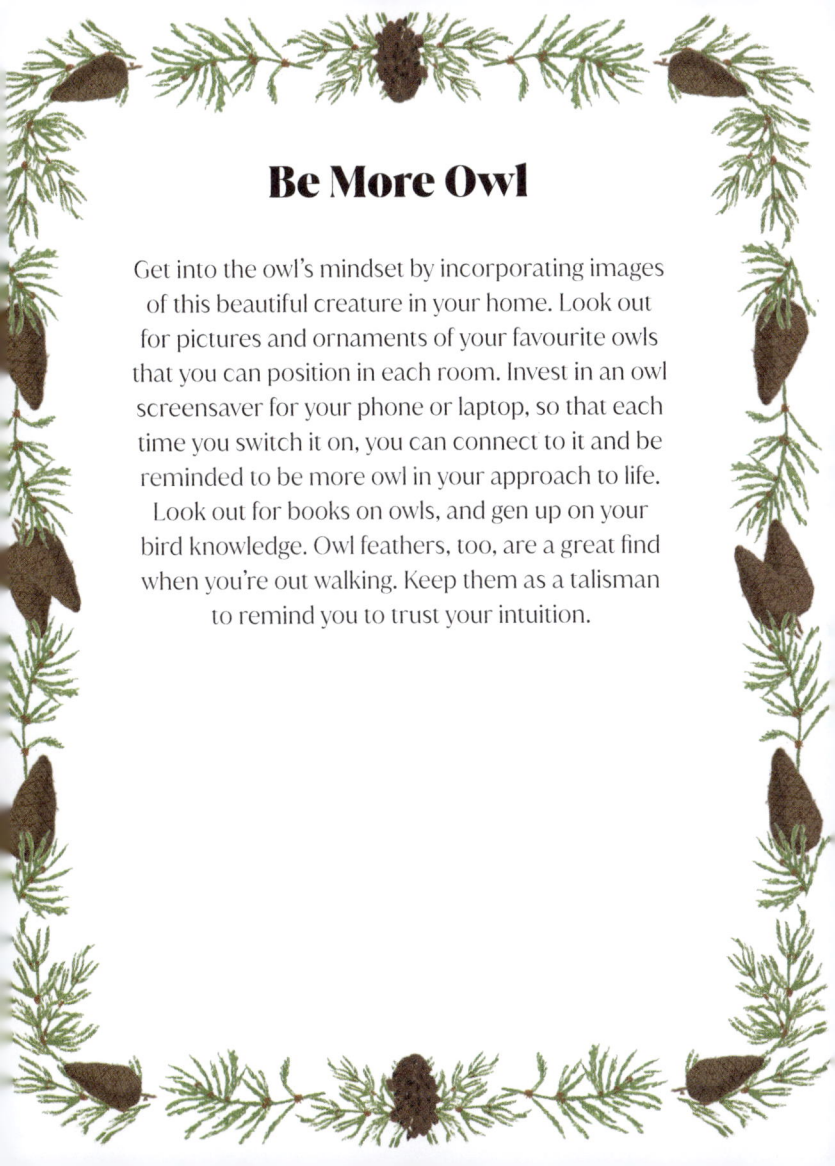

Get into the owl's mindset by incorporating images of this beautiful creature in your home. Look out for pictures and ornaments of your favourite owls that you can position in each room. Invest in an owl screensaver for your phone or laptop, so that each time you switch it on, you can connect to it and be reminded to be more owl in your approach to life. Look out for books on owls, and gen up on your bird knowledge. Owl feathers, too, are a great find when you're out walking. Keep them as a talisman to remind you to trust your intuition.

Trigger Your Psychic Senses

Owls are naturally receptive, but we have to work a bit harder to read those subtle **signs and clues**. To help you open your mind and feel intuitively, try this exercise. You will need a scented candle – choose something that will help you relax, like lavender, sandalwood or ylang ylang.

Step One

Light the candle and watch as the flame bursts to life. Stare into the brightness and notice how it flickers and grows. Breathe deeply as you do this and feel your body and mind relax. Inhale the sweet scent and let it soothe you.

Step Two

Close your eyes and bring your attention to the space in the middle of your forehead. This is where the Third Eye chakra resides. This is the energy centre associated with psychic and intuitive thoughts and feelings. Imagine there is a flame sitting in this spot, and picture it steadily growing.

Step Three

Picture the flame now travelling through your neck and head until it emerges through the centre of your scalp. Imagine the flame growing in width and length; see it burning brightly, casting light in every direction.

Step Four

Know that the flame is an antenna, helping you pick up psychic messages and insights. It reaches out from your subconscious mind and connects you to the world around you. Sit with this knowledge, and continue to breathe deeply.

Step Five

Slowly, steadily, imagine the flame retreating back through the centre of your scalp. See it behind your eyes, in the middle of your forehead, and then take a deep breath in and as you exhale, imagine blowing it out.

Step Six

Relax and open your eyes. Let the candle burn down and enjoy the lovely aroma.

Be More Owl

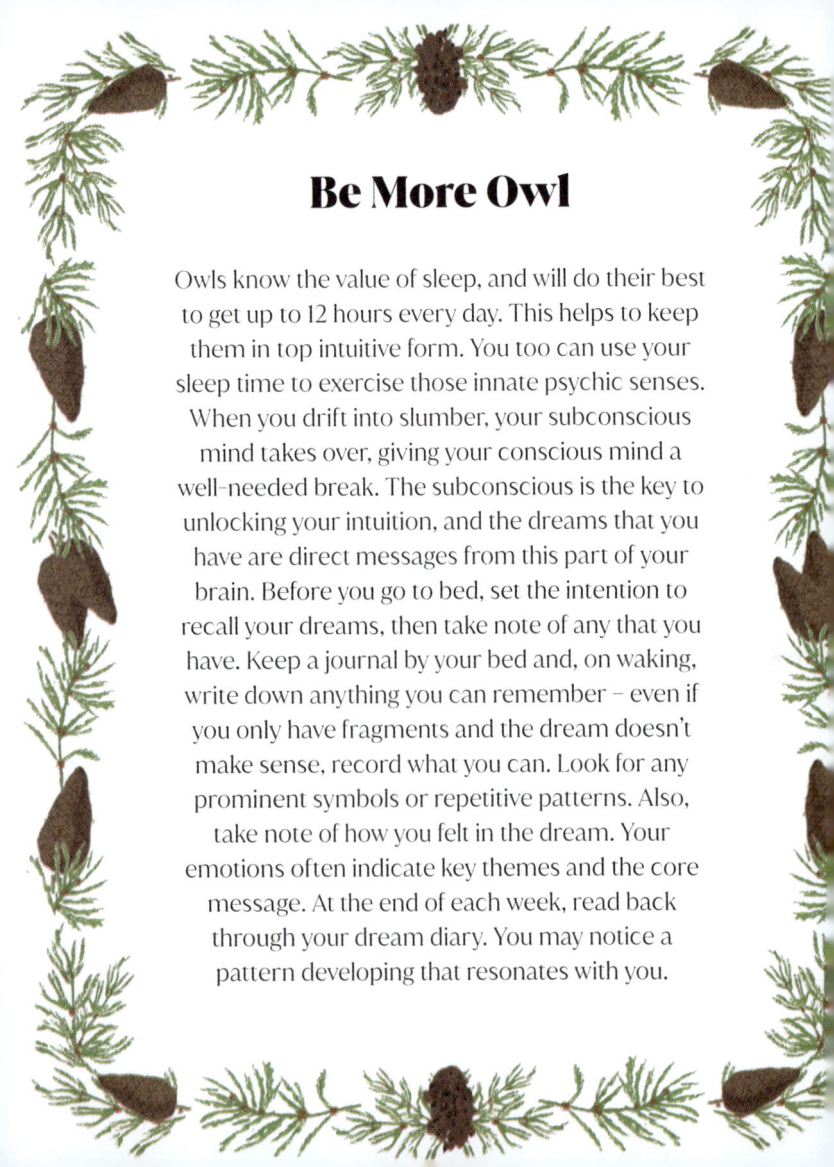

Owls know the value of sleep, and will do their best to get up to 12 hours every day. This helps to keep them in top intuitive form. You too can use your sleep time to exercise those innate psychic senses. When you drift into slumber, your subconscious mind takes over, giving your conscious mind a well-needed break. The subconscious is the key to unlocking your intuition, and the dreams that you have are direct messages from this part of your brain. Before you go to bed, set the intention to recall your dreams, then take note of any that you have. Keep a journal by your bed and, on waking, write down anything you can remember – even if you only have fragments and the dream doesn't make sense, record what you can. Look for any prominent symbols or repetitive patterns. Also, take note of how you felt in the dream. Your emotions often indicate key themes and the core message. At the end of each week, read back through your dream diary. You may notice a pattern developing that resonates with you.

Let Intuition Be Your Guide

Owl Spotlight

Eurasian Eagle Owl

One of the world's largest owls, this **MIGHTY BIRD**, with a wingspan of around 180cm (6ft), is found throughout Eurasia. Known in German as the 'uhu', or sometimes called the eagle owl, it has pale underparts with upper feathers that are deeply mottled and a buff brown in hue. Large ear tufts and **bright orange eyes** sit within a grey facial disc. The Eurasian eagle owl favours rocky landscapes for breeding, typically seeking out cliff edges. This bird has a diverse habitat, and can be found in coniferous forests, grassland areas and desert edges.

Read the Signs

Every day, we are presented with signs and symbols that resonate with us through the power of synchronicity. These may seem like coincidences, but they can help to point us in the right direction and provide guidance. To develop your intuition, you must first take note of the signs that are presented to you and learn how to read them.

The following tips will help you work with synchronicity, and recognize key signs.

🌿 **Be aware**. Engaging all of your senses and staying present will give you the best chance of seeing and recognizing any signs presented to you.

🌿 **Stay open-minded**. Synchronicity is about recognizing coincidences, particularly when they have personal relevance. For example, you might have been thinking about broadening your knowledge in a particular area, then on your way to work you see a discarded leaflet for a course on that subject. This is a sign from the universe and an intuitive nudge in the right direction.

🍂 **Look for themes.** Recognize when certain themes or subjects recur in your life, particularly in a short space of time. For example, you might experience three or four conversations that centre around the same theme, and make you think more deeply upon it.

🍂 **Trust your gut.** Lean in to your emotions and how you feel inside. Recognize when something makes you sit up and pay attention. There is a reason for this, and it's likely that it's a sign that you have intuitively homed in on.

Owl Magic: Psychic Stones

Deeply reflective, owls' eyes come in a range of colours, from the **CITRUS-BRIGHT HUES** of the snowy owl to the black-as-night orbs of the tawny. The one thing they all have in common is a discerning gleam, which is profoundly hypnotic. To help utilize your psychic senses and tap into your inner wisdom, make the owl your magical familiar by investing in a stone that matches the eyes of your favourite species. Those with darker eyes might choose a piece of obsidian or tourmaline, both of which are associated with insight, intuition and protection, while a brighter, lighter choice might be a piece of amber or golden citrine. These stones promote energy, and help you connect with the world around you. Keep your stone of choice with you as a charm to boost psychic awareness. When you need insight or guidance, **hold it in both hands and breathe deeply** while asking for a message. You can also place the stone under your pillow at night, to promote prophetic dreams.

OWL AFFIRMATIONS

I am open and ready to connect
with the world around me.

My thoughts and feelings provide psychic insights.

I tune into my intuition and let it
guide me through each day.

My inner wisdom grows with each breath I take.

I trust my intuition;
I have all the answers I need within me.

Synchronicity is the magical force at work in my daily life.

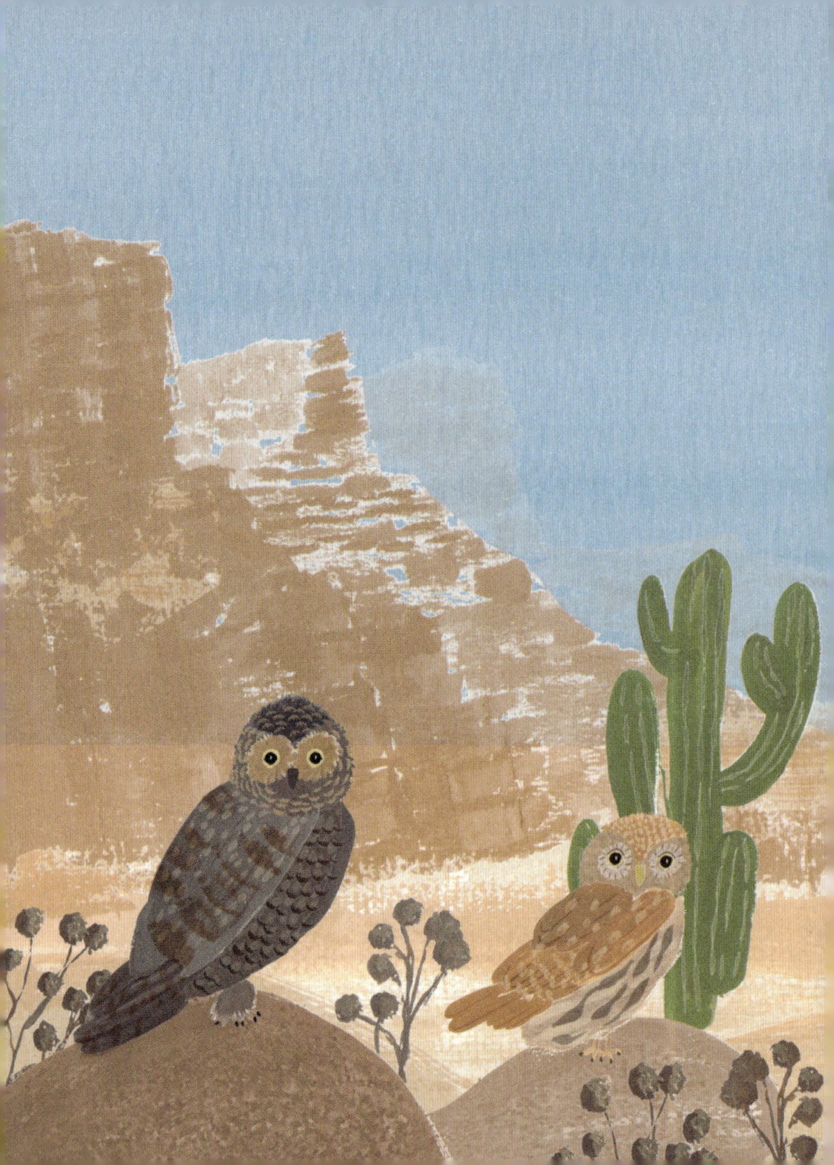

Chapter Six
Embrace the Darkness

'If we cannot sing of faith and triumph, we will sing our despair. We will be that kind of bird. There are day owls, and there are night owls, and each is beautiful and even musical while about its business.'

Henry David Thoreau

Either side of dusk or dawn, when shadows play across open meadows, **a creature of the night emerges**. Silent and stealthy in flight, its haunting cry splits the air in two and for a moment it seems that all the world is awake and hoping that the plaintive call is not for them. Doom follows in its wake – at least that's what they believed in times of old. Owls, for their misfortune, have long been seen as **HARBINGERS OF GLOOM**. Linked to all things evil and mysterious, they were the consorts of witches; demonic beings who lurked in the night causing mayhem and mischief. Some even believed that they were witches who had shifted into feathery form, and that their call was a curse laid upon the heads of innocent sleepers.

It's easy to see why they gained such a sinister reputation. A combination of nocturnal activity and their striking appearance was bound to conjure fear in those with a fervent imagination. Europe in the Middle Ages was a time of **great superstition**, when whims and fancies held meaning. Evil lurked around every corner and there were signs of this wherever you looked. For those with nothing better to do than point the finger, those creatures blessed with a dark side, be it dark colouring or a preference for the night-time hours, became fodder for gossip. After all, the devil was always close at hand and worked in **MYSTERIOUS WAYS**.

Many believed that if an owl flew over the roof of a house and issued its haunting call, then death would visit one of the occupants. In Germany it was considered bad luck to be born to the call of an owl, for while it might be nature's fanfare, it was thought to blight the child forever. Some African tribes attested that owls had the ability to steal souls, and also babies from their cots in the dead of night.

But just as owls could lay doom at your door, they could also repel negativity, according to some. Owl skins were often hung outside to keep **EVIL FORCES** at bay, while wearing the eye of an owl as a pendant was a popular fashion choice in Morocco, where it kept the Evil Eye away. Repentant Romanian souls craved the presence of the snowy owl, who would carry their spirit to the heavens, while Puerto Ricans preferred to keep their distance from the bird they termed the sinister 'múcaro', or **'eagle of the night'**. Thought to be a thief in the night, this fiendish owl would steal coffee from the mountain plantations, leaving them bereft and caffeine-less in the morning.

As far-fetched as these superstitions may seem, the owl still has an air of mystery about it, as it traverses the **inky blackness of night**. Perhaps this is due to its habit of keeping to the shadows – but in truth, this bird prefers the darkness. Its large eyes take in more light than most and it uses this gift well to see things that others might miss.

Embrace the Darkness

There is beauty in darkness. The owl knows this and is empowered by the shadows. This talented predator knows that while it's scary to immerse yourself in the gloom, there is much to be gained from the experience. **LIFE IS ABOUT BALANCE** and while the light may lift us up, the dark has a purpose too.

As humans, of course, we don't need to hunt in the dead of night. But that doesn't mean we can't explore the darker parts of who we are to find harmony, ground ourselves and accept every part of our personality.

Be More Owl

Invite the darkness in and feel the benefits of its protective cover by waiting until the dead of night and turning off all the lights. Stand by a window and gaze out. Let your eyes acclimatize to the surroundings, just as the mighty owl sits in silence and lets the blackness unfold. At first you might not see much, but have patience and take your time. Stand and breathe in the vista. Soften your gaze and you will notice shapes taking form. If it helps, direct your gaze to the sky and pick out the twinkling stars. If it's a clear night, you might be able to make out constellations. Use the soft glow of the moon to illuminate your mind and help you see clearly. Notice how everything looks different under the cover of darkness. Things that you might normally recognize take on a new appearance and seem to shapeshift. Stand, breathe and relax.

Embrace the Darkness

Find Your Balance

Owls are graceful creatures. They use their bodies to **glide through the night sky** with ease. Everything is in perfect balance. Whether they're hunting at dusk or dawn, or simply taking in the brightness of a new day, they approach the light and dark with an open heart and **FIND HARMONY** between both elements.

Try this!

You will need:
Some space where you can move freely, a yoga mat or a fairly soft surface.

🌿 To begin, stand with your feet hip-width apart. Elongate your spine and draw your tummy muscles in. Roll your shoulders back and tilt your chin up slightly.

🌿 Take a breath and bring your weight down into your knees, until they are bent and you feel the stretch along your thigh muscles.

🌿 Bounce lightly in this position, keeping your back straight. Settle into a comfortable position with your legs bent.

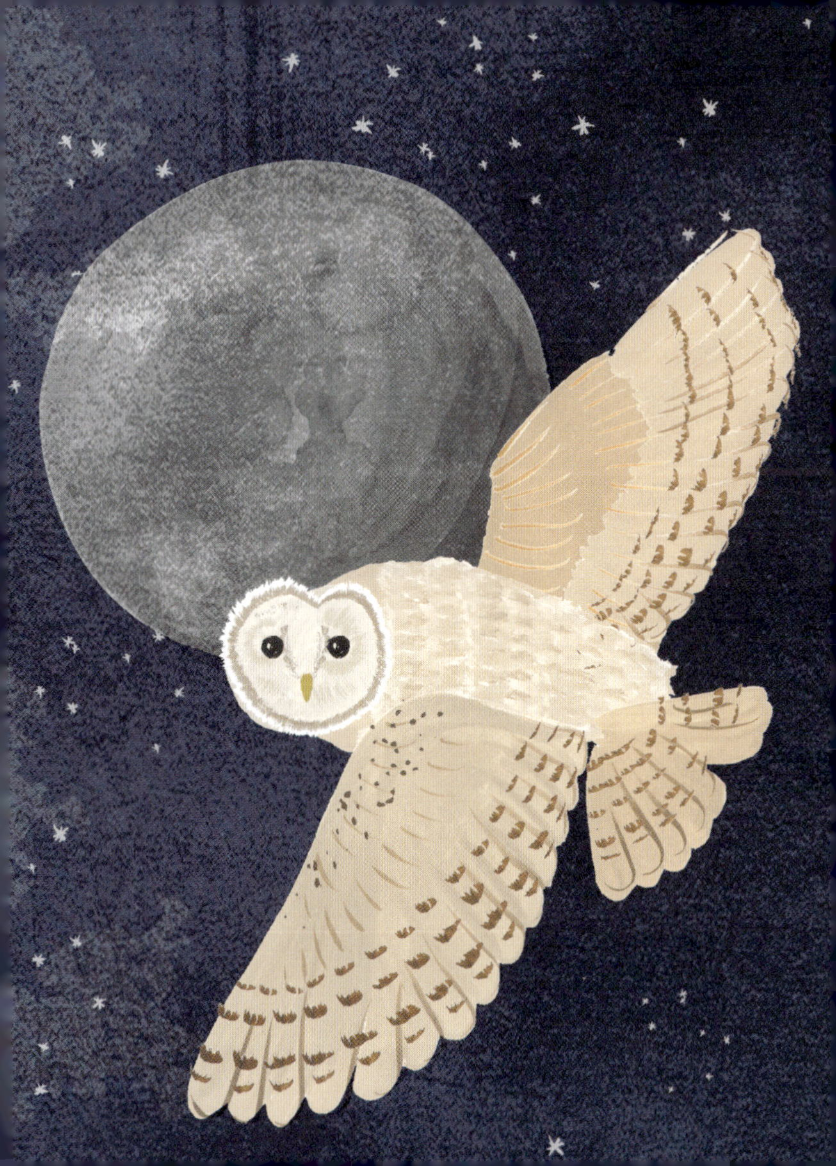

Embrace the Darkness

🌿 Slowly swing to the right from the waist with your arms outstretched. Imagine this is the 'light' side: it represents the day and the joyful light of the sun.

🌿 Now slowly swing to the left. This is the 'dark' side and represents the night, and the soft glow of the moon.

🌿 Continue to steadily swing between both sides for a couple of minutes, twisting at the waist and stretching as far as you can go.

🌿 Feel the point of balance when you return to the centre, with your legs still bent, and take a moment to breathe into this space.

🌿 To feel in perfect harmony, you need to be able to move easily and freely from light to dark, but always remain balanced and grounded.

Be More Owl

Acknowledge and accept the darker side of your emotions. As humans we often try to bottle up negative feelings, believing it's better to keep them inside, but this does us more harm than good. The canny owl knows to screech it out, to let the night absorb the darkness and feel a sense of freedom as all of the fear and negativity is released. Throughout your day, check in with yourself and notice how you truly feel. If you're feeling angry, frustrated or stressed, acknowledge this. Find a quiet place where you can stand and release the emotion. Say either out loud or in your head, 'I'm angry/frustrated/fearful/hurt' and say it with feeling. Let those emotions infuse your words. Repeat the phrase until you feel you've fully accepted it, and let some of the harmful feelings go. Breathe deeply as you do this, and try to release the feelings in your outward breath.

See Light in the Darkness

Owls know the benefits of working with day and night. They **embrace both sides equally**. Balance all aspects of your personality with this exercise that will help you see that there is **light in the darkness**. You will need a pen and some paper or a journal, and some time to reflect.

Step One

Down the length of the paper, draw two lines so that you have three columns, equally spaced.

Step Two

In the first column write down all your positive traits and characteristics, using a few words for each, such as 'I am cheerful', or 'I'm a good listener'. If you're struggling to do this, try and recall compliments that you have received, or ask a friend to help you.

Step Three

Now consider any negative traits and write those down in the second column. For example, you might say 'I am a worrier', or 'I can be impatient'.

Step Four

In the final column, consider each of the negative comments and put a positive spin on it. For example, if you said 'I'm a worrier', then in this column you might say 'I care deeply about everything'. If you said 'I can be impatient', you might write 'I am driven'. Do this with every one of the negative traits, if you can.

Step Five

Read through all of the lists and you will see that even the qualities that you think aren't so favourable have a positive side, and that they work together with your other strengths and gifts to make you whole and balanced.

Step Six

Keep adding to all of the lists, as and when you think of new traits, but always remember that in the darkness there is always an opportunity to move forwards and create something positive.

Be More Owl

To fully embrace the light and dark in life, we must also accept that others are a balance of these two halves. No one is perfect – we all have our flaws, and that's what makes us unique and magical. If you find yourself focusing on the negative aspects of a person, then consider why these strike a chord with you. Is it because you recognize these traits in yourself? Often the things that annoy us about others are a direct reflection of our own issues and challenges. When we see and recognize these negative aspects in others, we become instantly uncomfortable. Instead of focusing on their perceived flaws, consider the positive aspects of the person that balance this out. Remember that we are all diverse, and a combination of light and dark, and that's what makes us beautiful.

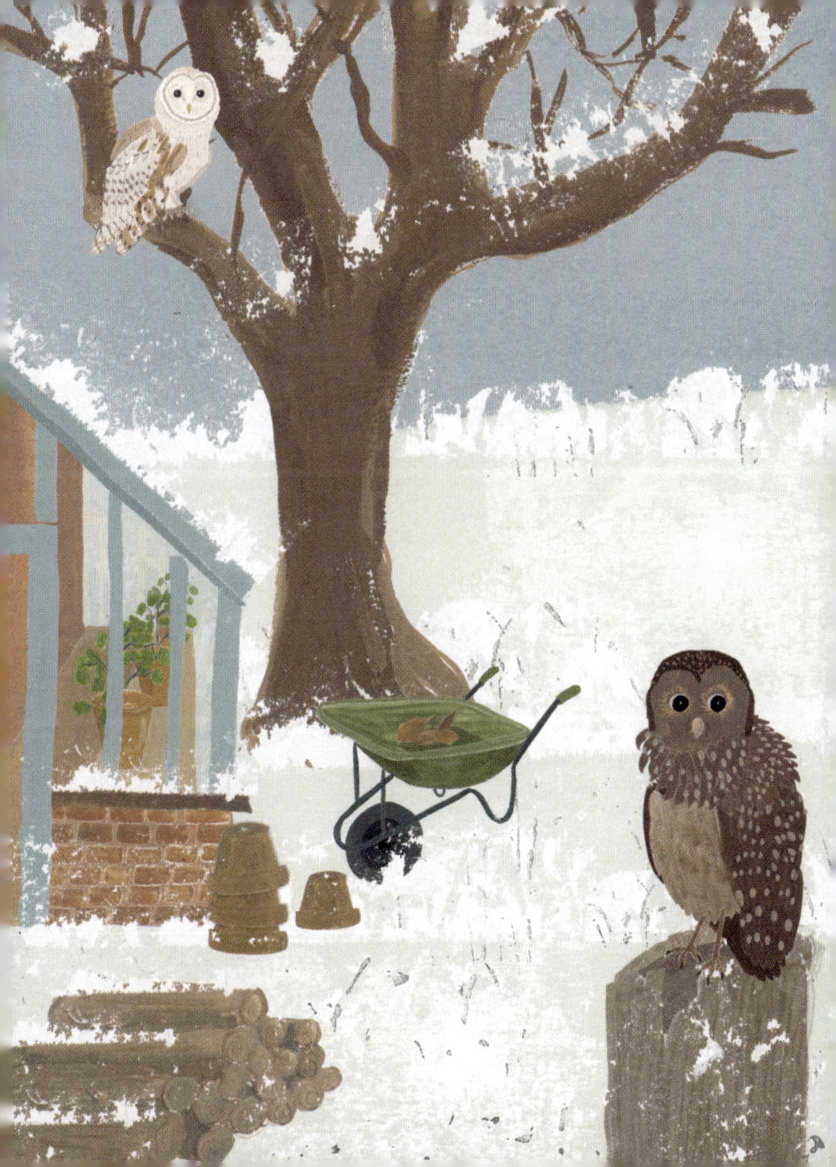

Embrace the Darkness

Owl Spotlight

Great Grey Owl

One of the longest owl species in the world, the great grey is around 61–84cm (24–33in) tall, with a wingspan of 1.5m (5ft). This owl has a large head and dense, **FLUFFY GREY FEATHERS** that coat the length of its body. A round, grey facial disc, with white patches around the eyes and a **MOUSTACHE-SHAPED CHIN STRAP**, make for a memorable exterior, giving this owl a discerning appearance. Distributed throughout North America, Scandinavia and northern Asia, these birds frequent boreal and coniferous forests.

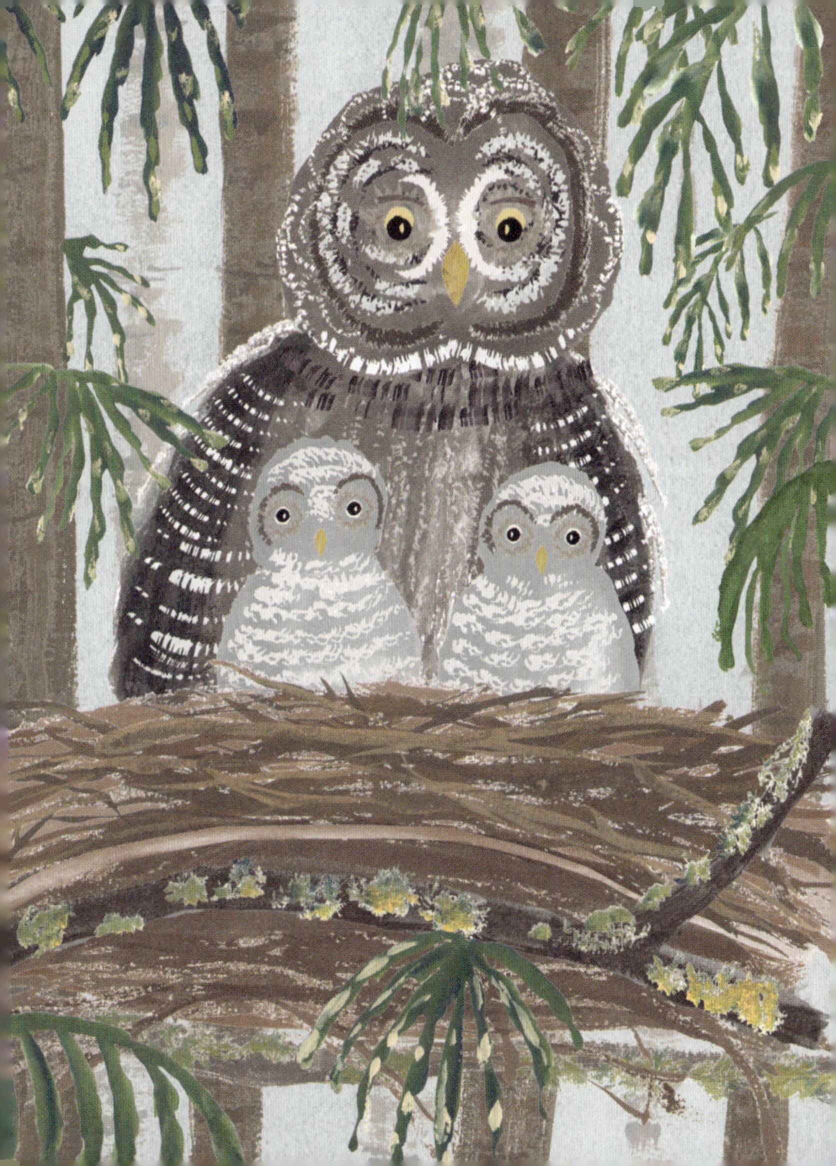

Become a Night Owl

Under a blanket of stars, everything looks different. The most familiar places become new and magical. If you're feeling like life has lost some of its sparkle, pretend you're a night owl and go for an evening jaunt. You don't have to go anywhere special; a stroll in your garden is enough to ignite your sense of wonder and put you at ease with the world.

🌿 **Wait until it's properly dark**, so that you can appreciate the magic of your surroundings fully.

🌿 **Stand outside and look up at the night sky**. Pick out the stars and the moon, and spend some time simply gazing at their beauty.

🌿 **Now look around you**. You can either take a gentle walk or simply appreciate the setting where you stand. Engage all of your senses as you do this.

🌿 **Notice the shapes** and how everyday things look different under the moonlight.

🌿 **Listen to the sounds of the night**. You might notice a faint shuffling sound as creatures move in the undergrowth, or city sounds in the distance. Let the symphony of darkness fill your senses.

🌿 **If you can't hear anything**, let the blanket of silence wrap around you.

🌿 **Notice what you feel, too**. Perhaps there's a slight breeze or it's chilly. Maybe the air is still warm upon your face. If you're feeling really brave, you might want to slip your shoes off and go barefoot in the grass.

🌿 **Drink in every part of the view**, and notice how different things look cloaked in shadow.

Owl Magic: Candle Spell

Find balance and harmony with a candle spell that you can do at night. You will need two different coloured candles of roughly the same size and shape. On one candle, carve a plus [+] symbol with a pin – this represents all of the positive aspects of your personality. On the other candle, carve a minus [-] symbol to represent any negative aspects. Place the candles next to each other, and light them both. Notice the flames of each, and how they grow and flicker at different rates, just as our emotions flare up and then gradually settle, allowing us to find balance. Repeat the following:

'Light and dark, a part of me.

Equal sides, my destiny.

Together these two make me whole,

balance and harmony are my goal.'

Relax and watch the flames burn for as long as feels right for you, then carefully snuff them out.

OWL AFFIRMATIONS

The dark of night casts a cloak of protection around me;
I am safe.

I stand with either foot in light and dark;
I am perfectly balanced.

I embrace the darkness within me, and work with it
to move forwards with grace.

Every day is an opportunity to find harmony within.

I am the sum of all my parts, and that's
what makes me whole.

The darkness absorbs my fear, the light ignites my passion.

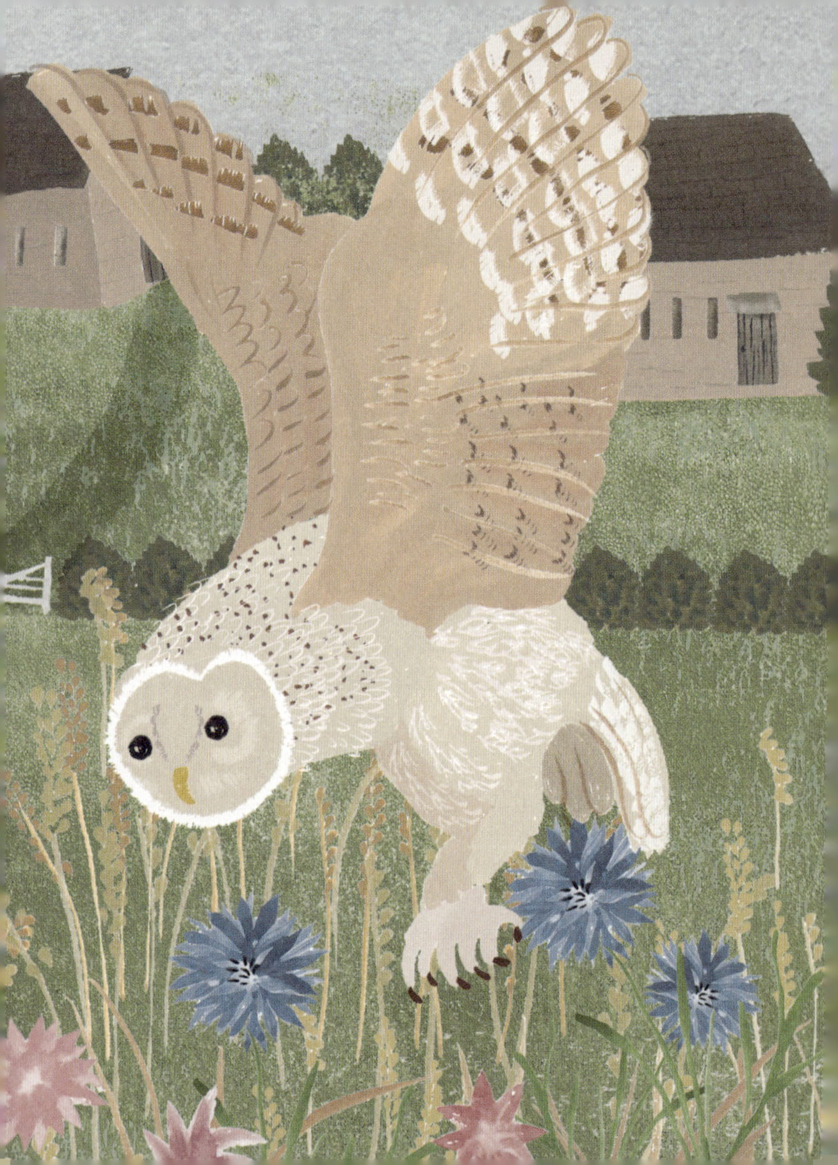

Chapter Seven
Release What No Longer Serves You

'The art of being wise is the art of knowing what to overlook.'

William James

Bite-sized snacks may work as a form of sustenance for us, but owls, like most other birds, prefer to swallow their prey whole. While this might sound greedy, these clever avians cannot chew and do not have a crop in which to store their foodie cache. Instead, each morsel passes directly from mouth to gizzard. No masticating needed, owls know that **true joy comes from diving in**, and should the prey be too big to down in one, then they make it more manageable by tearing off chunks until everything is gone.

LEFTOVERS ARE A NO-NO at any reputable roost. Each meal is precious and has taken time and energy to procure, so it is only respectful to pay attention when dining and clean your plate. That said, owls cannot digest everything they consume. Bones, fur and feathers are too hard to stomach and need to be eradicated to ease pressure on the digestive system – and help the owl process all of the good stuff. Just as in life, we need to **release the things that no longer serve us**, so that we can remain happy and healthy.

As you might expect from this wise and feathered wonder, its body is uniquely equipped to deal with anything harmful. The gizzard, which is a type of muscular stomach, takes care of the problem with ease. Fluids imbued with sand and grit combine to grind and dissolve anything of value into pulp, which is then broken down further to extract all of the nutritional benefits, while discarding anything that might hinder absorption. The nutrients are processed by the owl to **fuel its flight** and have even more adventures.

The discarded contents of the gizzard, which are usually bones, teeth and feathers, are then compacted into a neatly formed **PELLET**, a process that takes a few hours to complete after eating. While the bird definitely wants rid of the rubbish, it often stores it for around 20 hours, sitting with the excess until it is ready to release it gently through the oesophagus. This frees up space within the stomach chamber, and **VOILÀ!** The owl is ready to experience another gourmet feast, should one become available!

Of course, every bird is different and so is every pellet. Some are **tightly bound and oval** in shape, while others are **FURRY AND LOOSE** in structure. There are lengthy, misshapen monstrosities and then there are those works of art that appear to have been crafted by an owlish Michelangelo. The thing they all have in common is that they are surplus to requirements – done, dusted and delivered back to the earth in a convenient and recyclable package. How eco-friendly is that?

Owls have it sussed. They know that to **THRIVE AND SURVIVE**, they must also let go. They must shed what is of no use in order to reach new heights, and that means releasing stuff which may have had a purpose at first, but now weighs them down or is no longer safe to carry inside.

While they do this automatically, we can sometimes struggle with the baggage in our lives – but the method of regurgitation is the same. It takes time to sit in silent understanding, patience to digest and process what has passed, and courage to finally unburden yourself and **embrace a new, lighter way of being**.

But as any owl worth his wisdom will tweet – **'BETTER OUT THAN IN!'**

Be More Owl

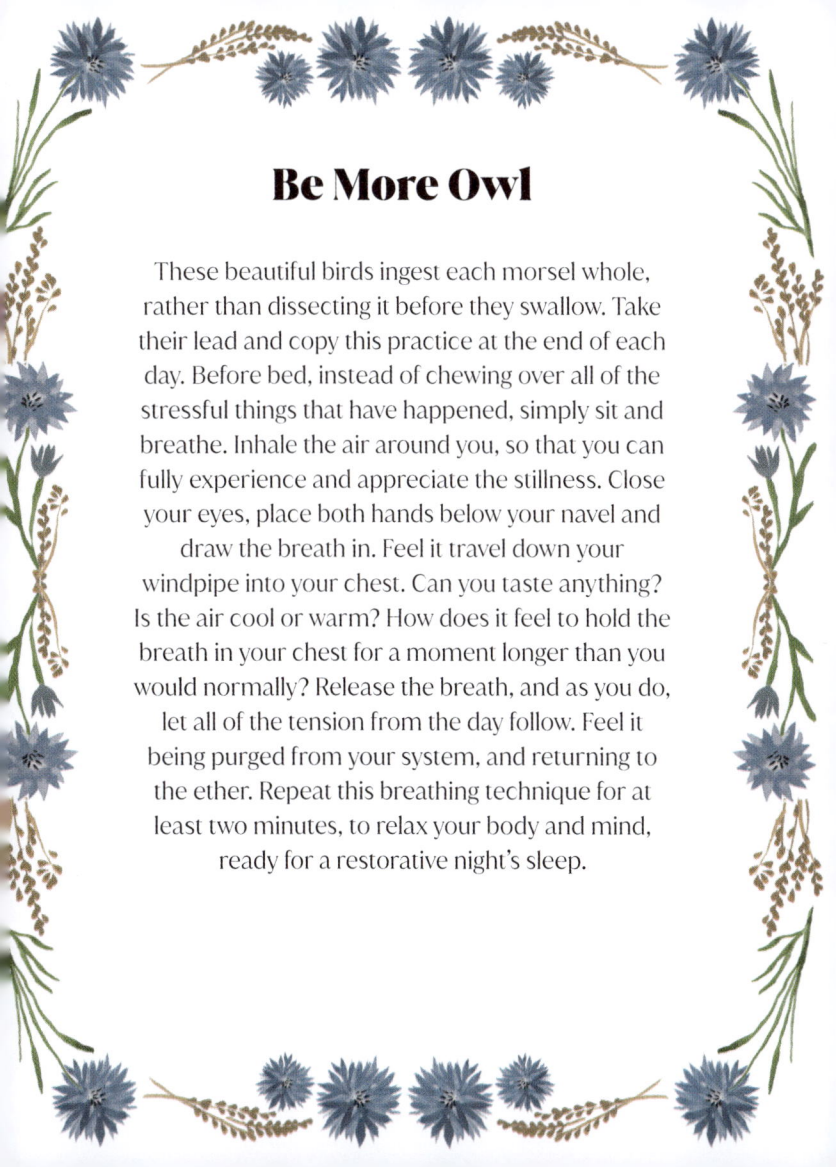

These beautiful birds ingest each morsel whole, rather than dissecting it before they swallow. Take their lead and copy this practice at the end of each day. Before bed, instead of chewing over all of the stressful things that have happened, simply sit and breathe. Inhale the air around you, so that you can fully experience and appreciate the stillness. Close your eyes, place both hands below your navel and draw the breath in. Feel it travel down your windpipe into your chest. Can you taste anything? Is the air cool or warm? How does it feel to hold the breath in your chest for a moment longer than you would normally? Release the breath, and as you do, let all of the tension from the day follow. Feel it being purged from your system, and returning to the ether. Repeat this breathing technique for at least two minutes, to relax your body and mind, ready for a restorative night's sleep.

Sit With It

Owls have two stomachs: the glandular, which produces acids and mucus to separate the digestible parts of each meal, and the gizzard, the muscular stomach that produces the pellet. Once formed, the pellet moves to the glandular stomach where it sits for around **TEN HOURS**, so that the owl has time to digest all of the key nutrients it needs before finally expelling the unwanted material.

Time spent sitting with your thoughts is never wasted. In order to let go of things you no longer need, you must first reflect and take what you can from each experience. Look for the positive lessons in everything that has passed, and release the negative emotions.

Try this!

You will need:
A journal, a pen and some time and space alone.

🌿 Light a candle and find somewhere comfortable to sit.

🌿 Consider what is holding you back in life. Perhaps there is an experience, a person or a behaviour that no longer serves you. Summarize this in a sentence and write it down in your journal.

🍂 Close your eyes and let any thoughts or feelings rise to the surface. How do you feel when you think about this experience/person/behaviour? Write down any emotions or observations that come to the surface.

🍂 Ask yourself if this experience/person/behaviour has taught you anything about yourself? If so, write down what you have learned. For example, a toxic relationship may have taught you how resilient you are, or a stressful job may have made you realize that you need to work moments of inner peace into your day.

🍂 Now think about the future and how different you will feel without this negativity in your life. Let your mind wander and imagine how this will feel and what it will look like. You might already be there, living in that future, having left the negative situation behind. If so, give thanks for this and for what you have learned. Write down any observations or thoughts.

🍂 Finally, relax and reflect upon what you have learned.

🍂 Read what you have written and be grateful for any positive lessons that you can take forward into the future.

🍂 Watch as the candle burns down and breathe deeply.

Be More Owl

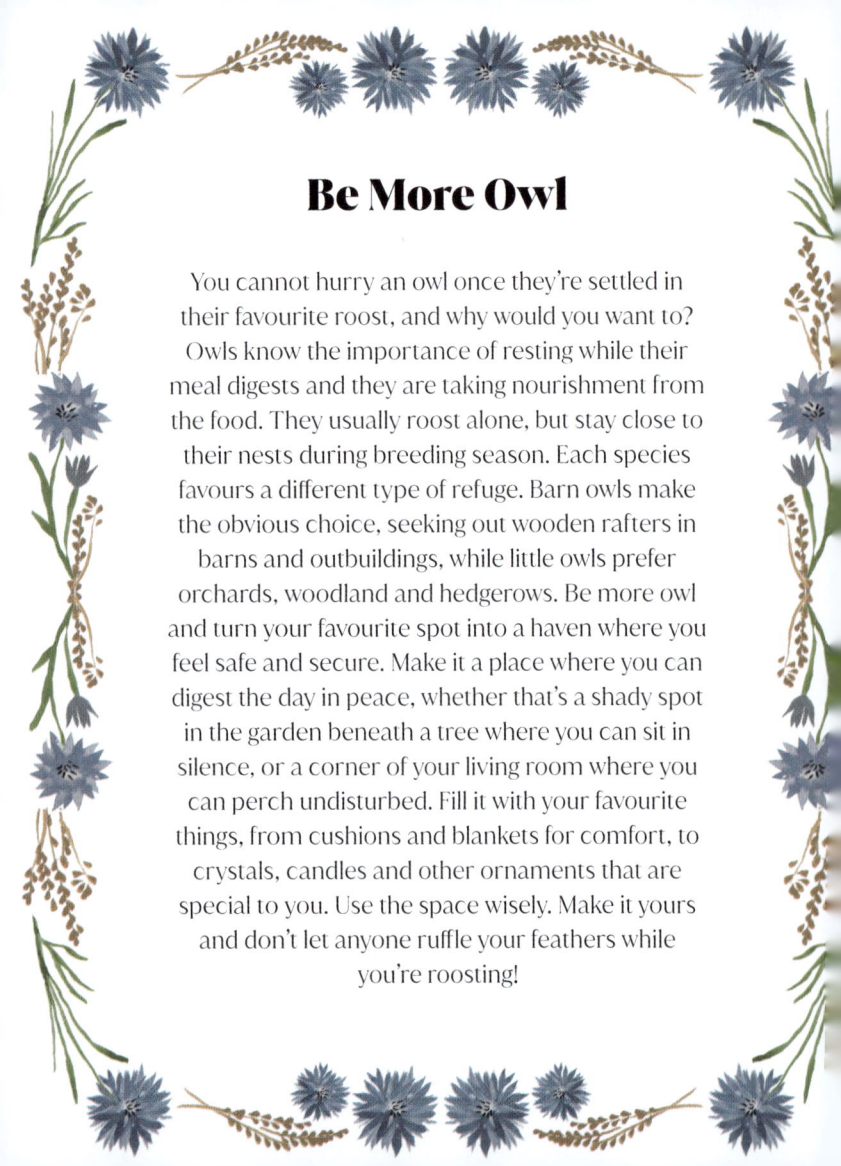

You cannot hurry an owl once they're settled in their favourite roost, and why would you want to? Owls know the importance of resting while their meal digests and they are taking nourishment from the food. They usually roost alone, but stay close to their nests during breeding season. Each species favours a different type of refuge. Barn owls make the obvious choice, seeking out wooden rafters in barns and outbuildings, while little owls prefer orchards, woodland and hedgerows. Be more owl and turn your favourite spot into a haven where you feel safe and secure. Make it a place where you can digest the day in peace, whether that's a shady spot in the garden beneath a tree where you can sit in silence, or a corner of your living room where you can perch undisturbed. Fill it with your favourite things, from cushions and blankets for comfort, to crystals, candles and other ornaments that are special to you. Use the space wisely. Make it yours and don't let anyone ruffle your feathers while you're roosting!

Paper Pellets

Unlike our feathered friends, you can't automatically regurgitate anything that is harmful to your wellbeing. This means you'll likely **hang on to negative emotions** far longer than you should. You'll carry them with you every day and, like any kind of luggage, this will eventually weigh you down. To truly fly free, you first need to find a way to release the excess baggage. This will help you feel lighter, brighter and ready for new adventures.

Try this step-by-step exercise to release the weight in pellet-sized chunks!

You will need a sheet of paper and a pen, a small firepit or fireproof bowl, and some matches.

Step One

Sit quietly and think about how you feel right now, and the emotions that you carry with you. Are there any negative feelings that you would like to get rid of?

Step Two

Try and summarize these negative emotions in a word. For example, if you feel guilty about something in your past, the word you would choose is 'guilt'. If you're afraid of something happening, then your word would be 'fear'. You might find you have lots of different emotions, so try and find a word for each one and write them on the paper, one by one. Each time you finish a word, tear it off and roll it up into a tiny ball.

Step Three

When you're finished, you might have a small bundle of paper balls. Slowly drop them, one by one, into the bowl or pit. As you do this, say 'I let you go, I set you free. I am released.'

Step Four

Take the matches and light the paper. Watch as it burns and each negative emotion turns to ashes. You might want to repeat the affirmation as you do this.

Step Five

Once cooled, scatter the ashes safely, either in a compost patch or your bin. Take a moment to reflect on how you feel right now. You might notice that you feel lighter in body and mind. Breathe and relax.

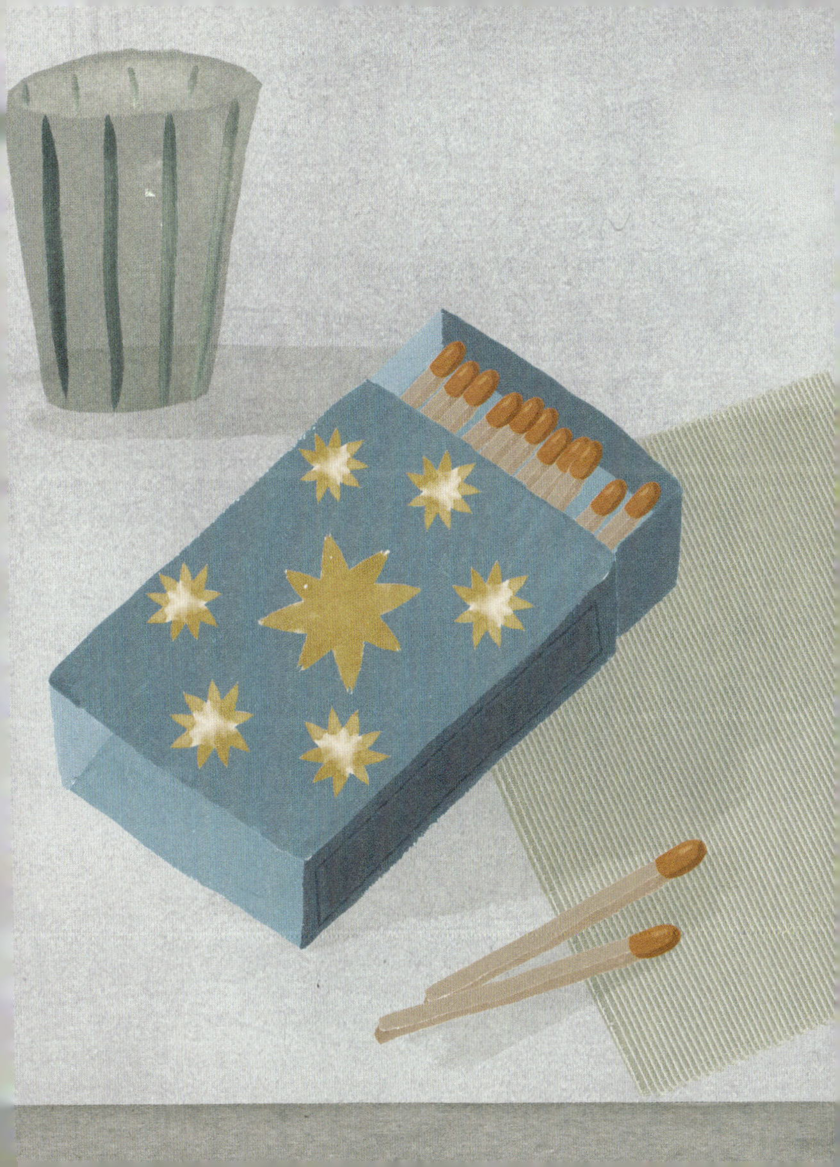

Be More Owl

Sharing how you feel can be a big help when you're trying to release emotions. It's not always easy to do this, and you need to be with someone you trust to open up in this way. If this isn't possible, try talking things out with yourself. Sit down somewhere quiet where you won't be disturbed, and imagine you are telling someone how you feel. Express your emotions and offload any fear or tension. Let out your anger, and shout, if you need to. If you find it hard to know where to begin, start by writing things down. Get everything onto paper, then read it out loud, venting all of your emotions as you do so. This will help you expel any negativity, having the same cathartic effect as regurgitating a pellet of all of the bad stuff that you want rid of.

Release What No Longer Serves You

Owl Spotlight

Burrowing Owl

This small, sandy-coloured owl has bright yellow eyes and **long, lanky legs**. A short tail and no ear tufts complete the look, giving this bird a quirky appearance. It gets its name from its habit of **COMMANDEERING BURROWS** from small mammals, which it then uses to live in. Active during the day, the burrowing owl favours open, dry spaces like grasslands, prairies and deserts, and can be found in North and South America.

Take Flight!

Wise owls know that there is a time for everything: hunting, eating, resting and digesting, regurgitating and taking flight once more. It's a repetitive cycle, but one that serves these winged beauties well.

Take inspiration from this regime and, when the time comes and you have released anything that has been holding you back, be ready to spread your wings.

🪶 **Seize the day**, with your arms wide open.

🪶 On rising, **throw the curtains back** and embrace the light with a stretch upon your tiptoes.

🪶 **Tilt your head upwards** and lengthen your spine.

🪶 **Tuck your tummy in** and reach wide with your arms, ready to grasp the air that surrounds you and draw it in.

🪶 **Inhale deeply** and feel the breath flooding your body with energy.

🪶 **Exhale and take flight** – imagine you're about to launch yourself into the day ahead.

🪶 You have found your wings and now **you can fly**!

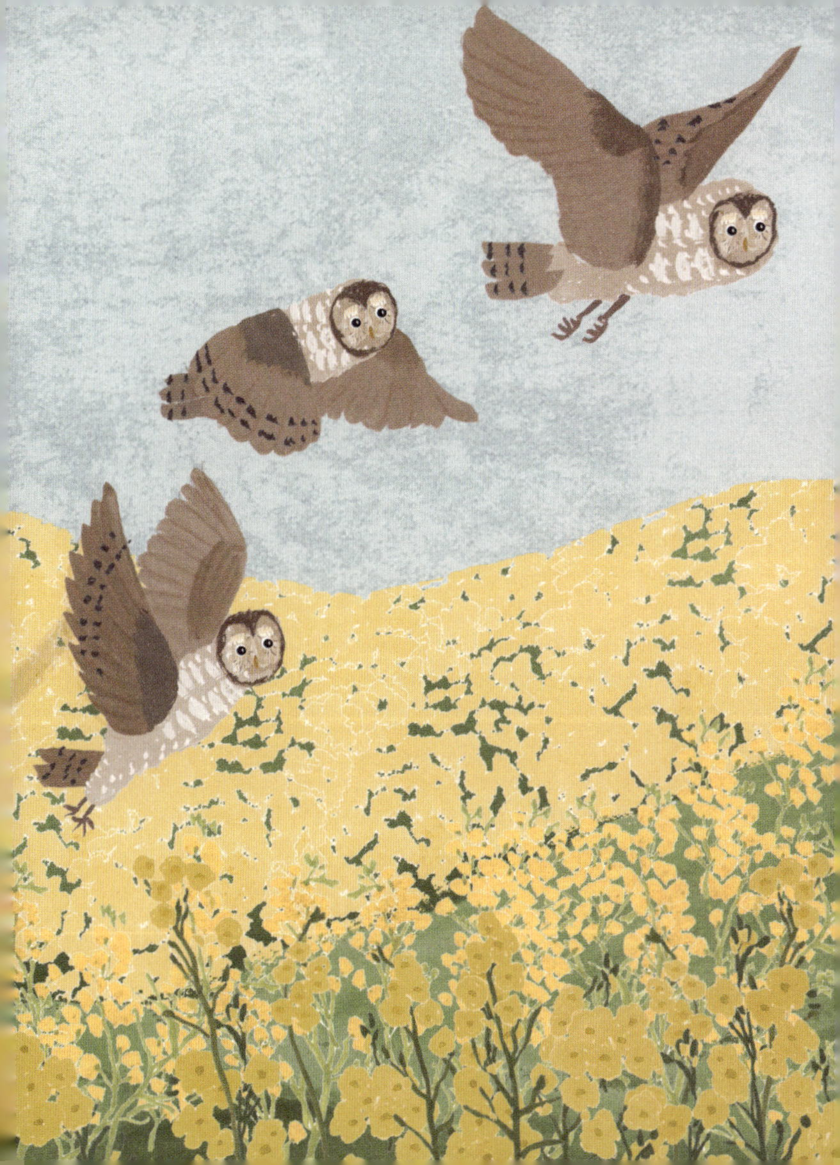

Owl Magic: Feather Cleanse Ritual

Since the dawn of time, feathers have been used in cleansing rites and rituals. Being linked to the air and the bird they came from, they are associated with **POWER AND FREEDOM**. Owl feathers are particularly potent. Associated with intuition and spiritual energy, they were often worn by both Celtic clan chiefs and Native Americans, and were used to connect to the spirit realm. If you can, get hold of an owl feather. If not, a large feather from another bird will suffice. Burn some sage essential oil in an oil burner or, if you prefer, take sprigs of fresh sage and place them in a small bowl of hot water. Use the feather to waft the scented air or steam around your body, and as you do this say: **'Negative energy fly away! I let you go, upon this day!'**

OWL
AFFIRMATIONS

I release my past and any guilt or fear
I carry with light and love.

With every breath I take,
I let go of tension, stress and pain.

My past does not define my future;
each day is a new beginning.

I release my grip on the things that no longer
serve me or weigh me down.

Each time I let go, I am renewed.

I am lighter, brighter and ready for new adventures.

Summary

As the pages of this book attest, **owls have something special**. It's more than just the way they look, or the numerous assets that they use to their full potential. It's an aura they carry with them – a mystical energy that radiates from their steady gaze and the way they hold themselves. Poised yet passive, they sit composed, able to blend into the environment as if wearing a cloak of invisibility. No need for magic tricks here; the owl doesn't rely on cheap gimmicks to stand out from the crowd. Its presence speaks volumes, whether perusing the shadows or soaking up the still of the night, this is a creature of grace and guile.

If, like me, you are already hooked by the impressive beak and mighty talons, then you are not alone. Once this bird has cast its spell upon you, there is no going back – and perhaps this is the secret of the wise owl. Once you start to appreciate **the joy of being more owl**, you will feel a deeper kinship with this bird, and may even notice it cropping up in the most curious spaces and places. The signs and synchronicities will leap out like an owl about to swoop, and you will happily fall prey to its charms.

Take your owl experience further by helping these birds to flourish. You can do this by joining and supporting a local conservation group and helping to make the land accessible for these majestic birds. If you have the space and you live in the right environment, put up your own owl box and encourage small rodents nearby by creating a brush pile of twigs, grass trimmings and old leaves. Every bit of support you give will help the owls in your area continue to **SURVIVE, THRIVE AND CAPTIVATE** a new generation of enthusiasts.

About the Author

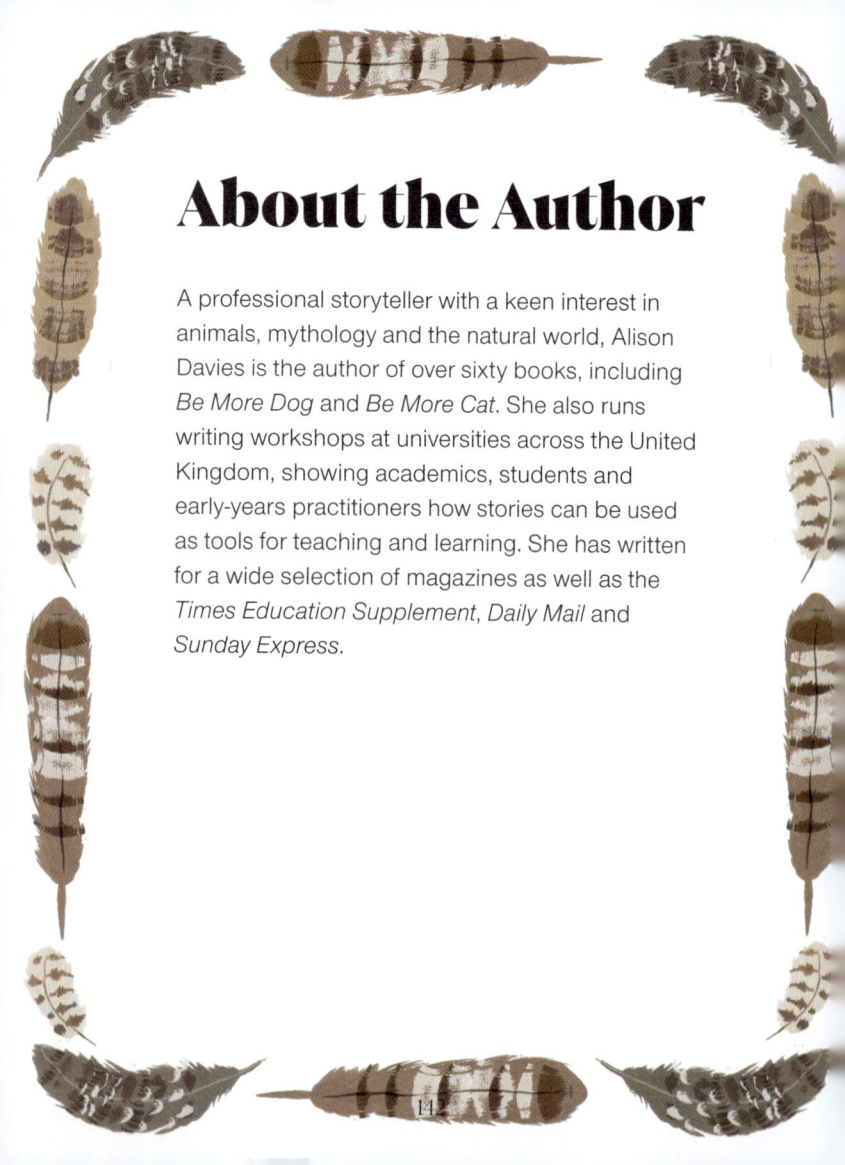

A professional storyteller with a keen interest in animals, mythology and the natural world, Alison Davies is the author of over sixty books, including *Be More Dog* and *Be More Cat*. She also runs writing workshops at universities across the United Kingdom, showing academics, students and early-years practitioners how stories can be used as tools for teaching and learning. She has written for a wide selection of magazines as well as the *Times Education Supplement*, *Daily Mail* and *Sunday Express*.

Acknowledgements

I would like to give special thanks to my brilliant editor Ellie Spence and the rest of the team at Quadrille, for the effort and care they have taken in creating such a beautiful book. I would also like to thank Emily Mayor for her fantastic illustrations. They capture the character and spirit of these enigmatic birds perfectly, and bring my words to life. We are so lucky to share the planet with such extraordinary creatures, and to have the opportunity to learn from them.

Quadrille, Penguin Random House UK, One Embassy Gardens, 8 Viaduct Gardens, London SW11 7BW

Quadrille Publishing Limited is part of the Penguin Random House group of companies whose addresses can be found at global.penguinrandomhouse.com

Penguin Random House UK

Text © Alison Davies 2025
Illustrations © Emily Mayor 2025
Design © Quadrille 2025

Alison Davies has asserted her right to be identified as the author of this Work in accordance with the Copyright, Designs and Patents Act 1988

Penguin Random House values and supports copyright. Copyright fuels creativity, encourages diverse voices, promotes freedom of expression and supports a vibrant culture. Thank you for purchasing an authorized edition of this book and for respecting intellectual property laws by not reproducing, scanning or distributing any part of it by any means without permission. You are supporting authors and enabling Penguin Random House to continue to publish books for everyone. No part of this book may be used or reproduced in any manner for the purpose of training artificial intelligence technologies or systems. In accordance with Article 4(3) of the DSM Directive 2019/790, Penguin Random House expressly reserves this work from the text and data mining exception.

Published by Quadrille in 2025

www.penguin.co.uk

A CIP catalogue record for this book is available from the British Library

ISBN 978 1 837 834 068

10 9 8 7 6 5 4 3 2 1

Managing Director Sarah Lavelle
Publishing Director Kate Pollard
Editorial Director Harriet Butt
Project Editor Ellie Spence
Design Manager Katherine Case
Illustrator Emily Mayor
Production Director Stephen Lang
Senior Production Controller Martina Georgieva

Colour reproduction by p2d

Printed in China by RR Donnelley Asia Printing Solution Limited

The authorised representative in the EEA is Penguin Random House Ireland, Morrison Chambers, 32 Nassau Street, Dublin D02 YH68.

MIX
Paper | Supporting responsible forestry
FSC® C018179

Penguin Random House is committed to a sustainable future for our business, our readers and our planet. This book is made from Forest Stewardship Council® certified paper.